THE BIG BOOK OF READING COMPREHENSION ACTIVITIES, GRADE 2

The Big Book of
Reading Comprehension Activities

GRADE 2

120 Activities for After-School and Summer Reading Fun

Hannah Braun, MEd

Illustrations by Joel and Ashley Selby

ZEPHYROS
PRESS

Interior and Cover Designer: Michael Cook
Art Manager: Sue Bischofberger
Editor: Mary Colgan
Production Editor: Erum Khan
Illustrations © 2019 Joel and Ashley Selby

ISBN: Print 978-1-64152-295-3

Contents

Letter to Parents and Teachers

As a parent and former teacher, I have spent a lot of time reading with kids. You know as well as I do that the magic of reading doesn't come from calling out all the words correctly. Reading is transformative when you understand the message the author is trying to send you. For kids, that means understanding why a story is funny, truly grasping a scientific concept, or seeing something familiar in a new way. Building reading comprehension is exciting and important.

If you have ever felt overwhelmed by reading standards, you are not alone. I've spent a lot of time unpacking the standards and finding ways to make them kid-friendly. I wrote this book to break those skills down into digestible pieces. As kids work through the activities, they'll build up their reading strategies and their confidence.

The book is designed around the following principles:

- Reading passages are relatable and interesting to kids.
- Kids get multiple, varied ways to practice strategies.
- The passages and skills are easier at the beginning of the book and get progressively more challenging.
- A variety of text genres is included.
- Each activity supports a standard or research-based teaching practice.

Each page includes a reading passage, instructions, and an activity. Answers for the activities can be found in the answer key toward the end of the book. You can start at the beginning of the book and move through it in order, or use the Skills Index and Common Core Correlations on page 129 to find activities that match a specific reading strategy or to find correlations to the Common Core standards.

These activities are designed to be completed with adult help, either one-on-one or in a small group in the classroom.

For kids that need more support, try the following:

- Give more help decoding words so the child can focus on comprehension.
- Read the text chorally (adult and child reading aloud together).
- Encourage the child to reread parts that were difficult.
- Think aloud to show how you interact with text. Use phrases like "This makes me think ...," "I noticed that ...," or "I wonder why...."

Kids that need a challenge may enjoy the following:

- Ask what they would do if they were the character.
- Make connections to other things they have read or seen.
- Say or write an alternate ending.
- Find additional books or websites about a topic of interest.
- Talk about what they found surprising or what changed their thinking.
- Ask if a lesson in a text might apply to something in their life.

I hope that you enjoy working on the activities in this book. It's exciting to think of all the ideas your child or student will be able to unlock as they apply reading comprehension skills throughout their life!

120 Reading Comprehension Activities

ANDY TO THE RESCUE ✓

Tweet, tweet.

Andy looked around the grocery store. What made that sound?

Then he saw it! Up in the beams, there was a bird.

It needed help to get back outside. Andy bought some bread. He put small pieces of bread in a line, starting below the bird and going out the door. Andy waited.

Soon, the bird flew down and ate the first piece of bread. It hopped to the next piece of bread. After a few more hops, the bird was out the door and flying away!

Color-code the reading passage according to the directions below.

The characters are the people and the creatures that are in a story.
Underline the characters in red.

The setting is where the story happens.
Underline the setting in blue.

What did the bird need?
Underline the answer in yellow.

How did Andy help the bird?
Underline the answer in green.

SKILL: Answer questions about key details

THE SEARCH FOR BABY BEAR

The Bear family was looking for bugs to eat in the woods.

"Hey!" said Mama Bear. "Where is Baby Bear?" Mama and Brother Bear looked behind a log. They looked around a big rock. They checked up in the trees. Baby Bear was missing!

Just then, they heard a splashing sound far away. They walked and walked until they got to some houses. They looked over a fence, and there was Baby Bear splashing in a pool!

Mama Bear was mad, but then she said, "It is a hot day. Let's all go for a swim!"

Sometimes the setting of a story changes from one place to another. Draw a picture of the setting at the beginning of the story and the setting at the end of the story.

woods

pool

SKILL: Answer questions about key details

IT'S TOO LOUD, MIGUEL! ✓

Miguel was playing drums in his room.

His brother said, "I'm trying to do my homework." Miguel took his drums downstairs.

Soon his dad said, "I have to make a phone call! Can you play somewhere else?" Miguel played in the backyard. Mr. Stevens from next door came outside.

"I know," said Miguel. "It's too loud."

"No," said Mr. Stevens. "There was a skunk living under my porch. I just saw it run away. Your loud drums got rid of that pest! Thank you!"

Miguel laughed and played some more.

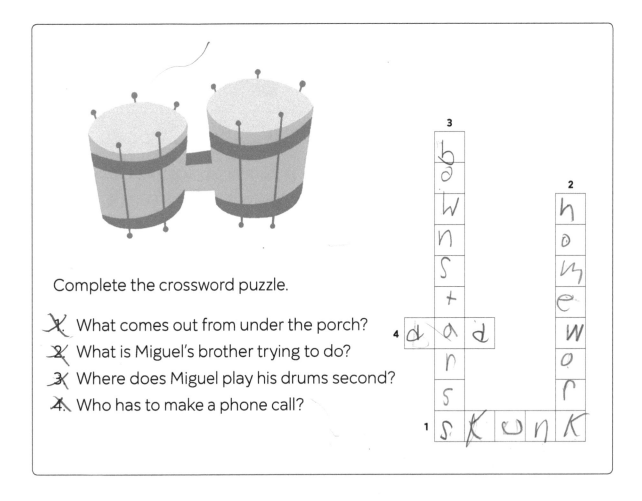

Complete the crossword puzzle.

1. What comes out from under the porch?
2. What is Miguel's brother trying to do?
3. Where does Miguel play his drums second?
4. Who has to make a phone call?

3 down: downstairs
2 down: homewor
4 across: dad
1 across: skunk

LEARNING TO PAINT

Kira wished she could make art. When she painted things, they didn't look real. One day there was a visiting artist who was painting in the library. Her painting didn't look like anything real.

Kira asked, "What is your picture going to be?"

The artist said, "This picture shows how I feel when I go walking by a pond." Kira didn't know you could paint a feeling.

At home, Kira made a colorful picture of curves and spots that showed her joy to learn that art does not have to look real.

Color the check if the statement is true or the X if the statement is false.

1. Kira saw an artist at the mall. ✓ ✗

2. Kira's pictures didn't look real. ✓ ✗

3. Kira learned about painting animals. ✓ ✗

4. Kira painted her feeling of joy. ✓ ✗

SKILL: Answer questions about key details

NEW SHOES

Rico saw the new Race Fast shoes at a store.

"I really want those!" he said.

"They cost so much!" said Rico's dad. "You need to make some money to help pay for them."

That night it snowed and Rico got an idea. The next day he went from house to house with his snow shovel. People paid him money to shovel their snow. By lunchtime he had made 20 dollars, but his feet were wet and cold.

"Are you ready to get those Race Fast shoes?" asked Rico's dad.

"No," said Rico. "I want to help pay for snow boots instead!"

Read the passage above to someone. Then use the tip of a pencil to hold a paper clip loop to the middle of the spinner. Flick the paper clip to spin. Ask a question about the text that starts with the word you land on. See if the person you read to can answer your question. Repeat several times.

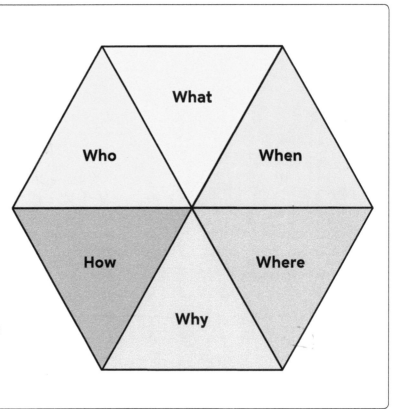

SKILL: Answer questions about key details

SARAH GETS TO WORK

Sarah's family sat down for dinner.

Sarah said, "I hate pork chops!"

"I spent a lot of time making this for you," said Sarah's dad. "You are being rude!"

Sarah didn't want to be rude, but she also wanted food that she liked. The next evening, Sarah got to work in the kitchen. She cooked noodles and made cheese sauce. She cut apples and set the table. It was hard work! Her dad sat down and looked at the food. What would he say?

"Thanks for making dinner, Sarah!" said Sarah's dad. His words made her feel good.

Stories have a beginning, middle, and end. Label the pictures with a B for beginning, an M for middle, and an E for end to match the story events. Can you use the pictures to tell someone else the events of the story in order?

e _____   b _____   M _____

SKILL: Retell stories, understanding the central message or lesson

A SLIPPERY SCIENCE PROJECT

DeShawn was hard at work making a penguin habitat in a box for science class.

He painted the box blue and white. It looked too flat. DeShawn added hills made of cotton balls. Now it looked too soft. DeShawn found some small rocks to add to his box.

The project still needed some animals. DeShawn added in some toy penguins and fish. The box was finished!

On Monday, DeShawn took it to school. The other kids all wanted to see what he had made.

"I love your project!" said Cory.

It was hard work, but DeShawn was glad he spent time getting everything just right!

Draw or write something that happened in the beginning, the middle, and the end of the story. Can you retell it to someone else using your pictures?

SKILL: Retell stories, understanding the central message or lesson

THE LOST BLANKET

Ziggy the dog loved his blanket. He carried it all over the house. One day, Ziggy's family got a new puppy. The puppy was always running and jumping.

I need a break from this puppy, thought Ziggy. He went outside. When Ziggy came back in, he couldn't find his blanket! It wasn't on the couch or on his bed.

"What will I do without my blanket?" howled Ziggy. Then he heard a snoring sound. The puppy was curled up with Ziggy's blanket. Ziggy was happy that the blanket helped the busy puppy sleep. Ziggy curled up next to the puppy and they both had a nice nap.

Start at the star. Color the arrows to make a path showing the story events in order.

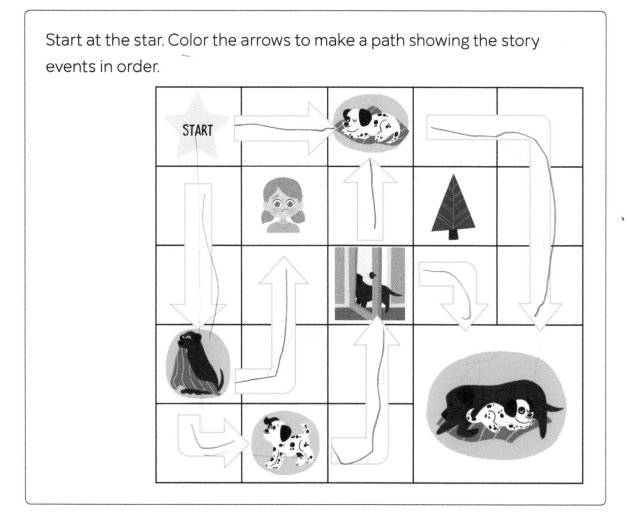

SKILL: Retell stories, understanding the central message or lesson

WHO WILL PLAY? ✓

On a warm day, Reesa took her sand toys to the park.

"Can I play, too?" asked a boy at the park.

"No! These are mine!" said Reesa. "Go play with something else!" The boy walked away. After a while, Reesa looked around because she heard laughing. The boy was playing a game with someone. Reesa had no one to talk to or play with. She was lonely.

Soon, a girl walked over. She looked at Reesa's sand toys.

"Want to dig with me?" asked Reesa.

"Sure!" said the girl. Reesa handed the girl a shovel and they worked together. Reesa had a lot of fun!

In many stories, a character learns a lesson. Write the words in the correct shapes to show what Reesa learned in this story.

At first, Reesa wanted to play by [h e r s e l f] . Then she started to feel [l o n l l y] . So she [s i d e d] a girl to play with her. Reesa learned that [p l a y i n g] can be fun.

SKILL: Retell stories, understanding the central message or lesson

MOVING AWAY

As Dustin rode away from his old house, a tear ran down his cheek. He would really miss his friends and his school. Dustin's family was moving to a new city. He wasn't sure how he could ever feel happy again.

When Dustin started at his new school, he saw a poster in the hall for an art club. Dustin loved drawing, so he decided to join. His last school didn't even have an art class.

One day, everyone in art club was drawing buildings. Dustin drew his old house. Thinking of the things he left made him sad. Then Dustin looked around at the friends he had made who were all doing something he loved to do. He smiled.

Write the words from the word bank on the shapes to show the lesson Dustin learned in the story.

Word Bank: joins a club   good things   happy   sad   moves away

Beginning

Event: Moves away   Dustin feels   Sad

End

Event: Joins a club   Dustin feels   happy

Dustin learns that even though change is hard, it can bring *good things*

SKILL: Retell stories, understanding the central message or lesson

A PLACE TO PLAY

Belle the beetle lived in a tree with her family. She had her friend, Bess, over to play Super Beetle.

"Super Beetle saves the day!" shouted Belle.

"Girls, you'll have to stop playing. It's time for the baby to take a nap," said Belle's mom. The friends walked out of the tree and sat on a branch. They felt sad. Belle's room was Super Beetle's hideout. How could they keep playing without it?

They went walking on the tree branches until they saw something new. It was an empty nest.

"This is the perfect hideout for Super Beetle!" said Belle.

"We never would have found it if we hadn't gone walking," said Bess. The beetles happily played and played.

Sometimes one action (a cause) can make something else happen (an effect). Draw a line to connect each cause with its effect.

Causes   Effects

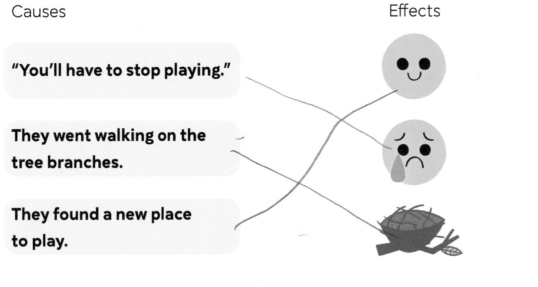

"You'll have to stop playing."

They went walking on the tree branches.

They found a new place to play.

SKILL: Describe how characters respond to major events

DIEGO STAYS COOL

It was a hot day. Diego was inside, playing video games with the fan on. Just then, the fan and the game stopped working. *The power must have gone out*, thought Diego.

"I'm so bored, Mom!" said Diego.

"There are lots of things that need to be done," said Diego's mom. Diego sat on the front porch, trying to think of something to do.

I wish I could jump into a pool to cool down, thought Diego. That gave him an idea. Diego turned on the hose. He sprayed water on his shirt. Then he watered the flowers. After that he washed his mom's car. Diego stayed busy and cool!

Use words or a picture to complete each cause and effect relationship from the story.

Cause

I wish I could jump into a pool . . .

Effect

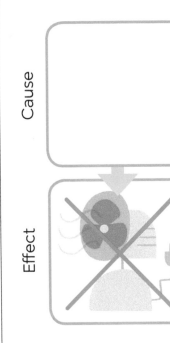

SKILL: Describe how characters respond to major events

THE SKY IS FALLING!

A drop of rain fell on Rick the chick's head.

"The sky is falling!" said Rick. He ran into the barn and bumped into a shovel. Chuck the duck felt a thud as the shovel hit the ground.

"The ground is shaking!" said Chuck. He slammed a gate as he ran to the barn. Pat the cat heard the sound.

"The trees are breaking!" said Pat. As she ran to the barn, she kicked up some dirt. Briggs the pig saw the dirt.

"The wind is dirty!" said Briggs. He ran into the barn. Just then the storm really started. The farmer looked outside. *Oh, good,* he thought. *The animals are already in the barn.*

Underline the text in the passage that answers each question using the color indicated.

1. What caused Briggs the pig to run into the barn? *Red*

2. What effect did the slamming gate have? *Blue*

3. What did the farmer do when the storm started? *Yellow*

4. Why did Rick the chick think the sky was falling? *Green*

SKILL: Describe how characters respond to major events

CARTER'S NEW TEAM

The Wild Cats had just won their football game.

"Wow, Carter!" said Coach Miller. "You got three touchdowns!"

"It's easy!" said Carter. "I hardly even have to try."

"Next week, I want you to play on the team with the older kids," said Coach Miller.

The next week Carter didn't get any touchdowns.

"Coach," said Carter. "All the kids are faster than me."

"Practice running every day," said Coach Miller.

Carter practiced running and the next game went better. Each week he got a little faster. By the last game, Carter got a touchdown! It had been hard work playing with the older kids, but Carter knew it had made him a better player.

Complete the crossword puzzle.

1. On his first team, Carter said playing football was easy

2. On the new team, all the other kids were faster than Carter.

3. Carter had to practice running.

4. Working hard to be on the new team made Carter a better player.

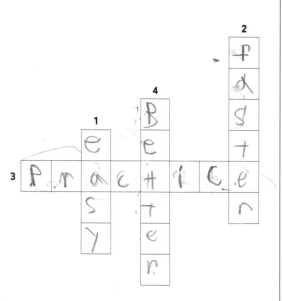

Practice

LITTLE RED   √

Little Red went to visit her grandma. On the way, she saw a wolf.

"Where are you going, little girl?" asked the wolf.

"Oh, hi!" said Little Red. "I'm going to my grandma's house. It's just up the path."

When Little Red got to the house, Grandma looked different. She had hairy ears and sharp teeth.

Just then, Grandma's cat jumped up and pulled off Grandma's hat. It wasn't Grandma at all. It was the wolf in Grandma's clothes! Little Red was scared!

The wolf was afraid of cats so he ran away howling. Little Red found her real grandma locked in the closet.

From that day on, Little Red never talked to strangers again.

Fill in the blanks to show how Little Red changed in the story.

In the beginning, I talked to a __wolf__.

The wolf dressed in __Grammas__ clothes.

I felt __scared__.

I learned not to talk to __strangers__.

SKILL: Describe how characters respond to major events

KEITH'S KITE

Keith went outside to fly his kite. After a few minutes, a big gust of wind pushed the kite into a tree. Keith pulled on the string but the kite was stuck. The only way to get it back was to climb the tree. Keith pulled himself up. The wind made the tree shake. Keith was a little scared but he kept going. He stepped on a branch that snapped beneath his foot.

Yikes, thought Keith. *I'd better be careful.*

He had to test three branches before he found a strong one that reached the kite. Keith never gave up. When he made it back down to the ground with his kite, Keith felt proud!

Color the check if the statement is true or the X if the statement is false.

1. The lost kite makes Keith feel sad.　　✓　✗

2. Keith gives up easily.　　✓　✗

3. Keith is brave.　　✓　✗

4. Keith cares a lot about getting his kite back.　　✓　✗

SKILL: Use illustrations and details in text to describe characters, setting, or plot

BOTS GONE BAD – PART I ✓

Cliffton was one of the most beautiful cities around. In other cities, you would find trash on the ground, but not in Cliffton. You could walk down the sidewalks between tall buildings and not see any stray paper. In the center of the city was a park. It had tall trees and lots of grass, but no trash. People came to eat from the food carts at lunch. When lunch was over, there were no napkins on the ground. Cliffton had a secret for keeping the trash under control.

Continued in Activity 18…

The setting of this story is a city called Cliffton. Write or draw three things you would see in Cliffton below.

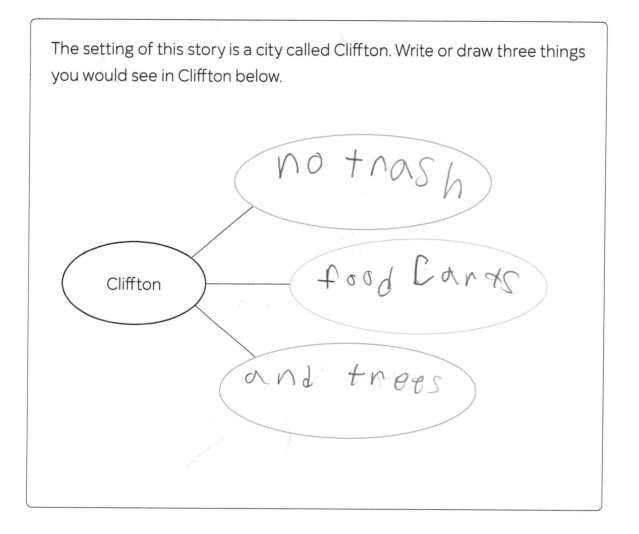

Cliffton

no trash

food carts

and trees

SKILL: Use illustrations and details in text to describe characters, setting, or plot

BOTS GONE BAD - PART 2

Continued from Activity 17...

Cliffton's secret was a new kind of robot. The Vac-Bot kept the city clean at all times. It rolled around on three wheels and drove over curbs, grass, and grates. The Vac-Bot had a big eye that helped it look for trash. When it found some, it used a broom arm to sweep the trash into its vacuum slot. A team of 10 Vac-Bots was able to pick up all the trash in Cliffton. The Vac-Bots worked perfectly until the day everything went wrong.

Continued in Activity 19...

Use the description in the text to draw a Vac-Bot.

SKILL: Use illustrations and details in text to describe characters, setting, or plot

BOTS GONE BAD - PART 3

Continued from Activity 18…

It was the hottest day Cliffton had ever seen. Kids were lined up at an ice cream truck. A boy dropped the paper wrapper of the ice cream bar he was eating. Right away, a Vac-Bot rolled up and began sweeping the wrapper into its vacuum slot. Just then, the Vac-Bot sparked. It was getting too hot in the sun. Smoke came out of the Vac-Bot and the Vac-Bot made a buzzing sound. The boy turned around to see what was happening. The Vac-Bot shot a puff of tiny paper scraps at the boy. It had taken the trash, cut it into pieces, and was shooting the mess all over!

As the other Vac-Bots got too hot, they also turned trash from one piece into lots of pieces. The people of Cliffton had to do something fast!

Continued in Activity 20…

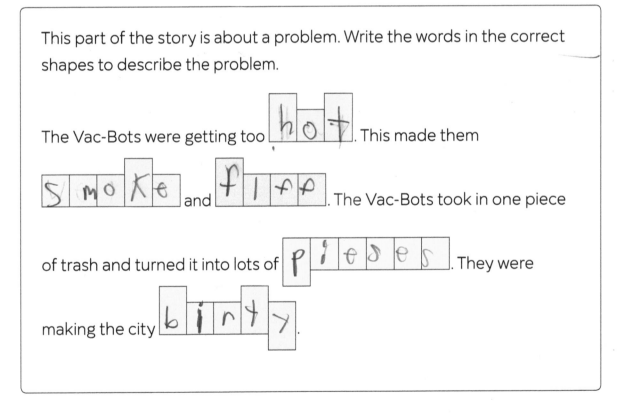

This part of the story is about a problem. Write the words in the correct shapes to describe the problem.

The Vac-Bots were getting too **hot**. This made them

smoke and **flip**. The Vac-Bots took in one piece

of trash and turned it into lots of **pieces**. They were

making the city **birty**.

SKILL: Use illustrations and details in text to describe characters, setting, or plot

BOTS GONE BAD - PART 4

Continued from Activity 19 . . .

No one knew how to turn the Vac-Bots off. The ice cream truck's music came on and a Vac-Bot turned toward it. As the truck drove away, the Vac-Bot followed it. The Vac-Bot seemed to like the music! The driver saw what was happening. She drove around the city until all the Vac-Bots were following her. The ice cream truck driver drove the truck into a big shed. All the Vac-Bots followed. She closed the door of the shed.

The city of Cliffton was now safe from the broken bots, but they also had to start picking up their own trash.

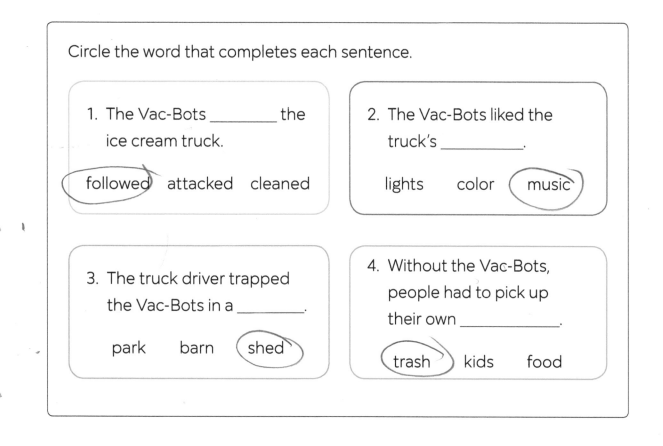

Circle the word that completes each sentence.

1. The Vac-Bots _____ the ice cream truck.

   (followed)   attacked   cleaned

2. The Vac-Bots liked the truck's _____.

   lights   color   (music)

3. The truck driver trapped the Vac-Bots in a _____.

   park   barn   (shed)

4. Without the Vac-Bots, people had to pick up their own _____.

   (trash)   kids   food

SKILL: Use illustrations and details in text to describe characters, setting, or plot

EARTH'S BIGGEST ANIMAL

The biggest animal on Earth lives underwater. It is the blue whale. Blue whales can grow to be about as long as three buses. They are found in all of the oceans around the world. These large animals are not fish. They breathe air. Blue whales have to come to the top of the water and use their blowholes to breathe.

Blue whales are big, but their food is very small. They eat little sea animals called krill. Blue whales can live for 80 to 90 years.

Write at least one detail from the text in each section of the chart below.

BLUE WHALES NEED . . .	BLUE WHALES CAN . . .	BLUE WHALES LIVE . . .
air to breathe.	Grow up to 3 busies.	In the ocean

SKILL: Ask and answer questions about key details

MUSCLES KEEP US MOVING

Muscles keep the body moving. People need muscles to walk, lift things, and even push food through their bodies. Muscles are made of many tiny cells. Sometimes you choose to use your muscles, like when you pick up your backpack. There are other muscles that move without us thinking about it. The heart is a muscle that keeps moving, or beating, even if you are asleep. It works harder than any other muscle in your body. Muscles get stronger when you use them. You can keep your muscles healthy by exercising.

Write the missing word in the blanks. Use the shapes below the blank spaces to find the letters that complete the last sentence.

1. When you use your muscles, they get s t r o n g e r .

2. Your heart beats even when you are a s l e e p .

3. Muscles help P U S h food through the body.

4. Muscles are made of c e l l s .

The muscle that works the hardest is t h e h e a r t .

LEARNING TO FIGHT FIRES ✓

People who want to be firefighters have many things to learn first. They go to special fire schools. They do exercises to get stronger and faster. Firefighters have to be strong to carry heavy tools and get up ladders and stairs quickly. They spend time in classrooms to learn about fires and safety. Fire schools also teach people how to take care of others that are hurt. At fire school, firefighters learn how to use big ladders, hoses, and (trucks). It takes three to four months to finish fire school. All of this training gets new firefighters ready to save lives!

Each sentence below has a piece of information that is wrong. Use what you learned in the passage to cross out what is wrong and write in a correction.

✓ Lessons about ~~cooking~~ *fire* and safety are taught at fire school.

Firefighters carry heavy ~~animals~~ *tools* up ladders.

Firefighters learn to use equipment like ladders and ~~computers~~ *trucks* at fire school.

✓ Fire school lasts three to four ~~days~~ *months*.

SKILL: Ask and answer questions about key details

WORLD'S FASTEST ANIMALS

Some animals are made to go fast. Animals that run fast are usually trying to catch food or trying not to become food! The fastest animal in the world is the cheetah. Cheetahs have to run fast to catch gazelles for food. Gazelles run a little slower than cheetahs. Lions also chase gazelles, but run slower. Lions run about 50 miles per hour. A smaller animal that can run fast is the rabbit. It can run about 35 miles per hour. Rabbits don't run to catch food. They run so they don't get caught! Humans are slower than all of these animals. The fastest a person can run is about 28 miles per hour.

Each bar on the chart represents an animal's speed. Using the information in the reading passage, label each bar with the correct animal.

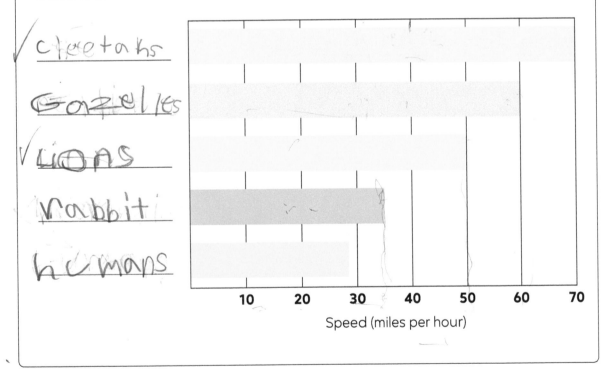

cheetahs

Gazelles

Lions

rabbit

humans

10   20   30   40   50   60   70

Speed (miles per hour)

SKILL: Use text features to locate key facts

CHOOSING HEALTHY FOODS ✓

Eating healthy food helps your body grow and do the things it needs to do. There are five different groups of food that you should choose from each day. In the grain food group are breads, rice, and noodles. In the vegetable group are foods like carrots, green beans, and lettuce. The fruit group includes foods like bananas, melons, and apples. Meat, beans, eggs, and nuts are in the protein group. The dairy group contains foods like milk, yogurt, and cheese. Eat a few servings from each group every day to stay healthy.

FOOD GROUP	SERVINGS PER DAY FOR KIDS
Fruits	2–3
Vegetables	2–3
Grains	6–11
Protein	2
Dairy	2–3

Based on recommendations found on the American Academy of Pediatrics website, HealthyChildren.org.

Use the table above to answer the questions.

1. Which food group should you have the most servings from? __Grains__

2. How many servings of vegetables should a kid have each day? __3–2__

3. Which food group do you need more servings from, fruit or grains? __Grains__

4. A cup of milk is one serving. Would a cup of milk give you all the dairy you needed for a day? __no__

SKILL: Use text features to locate key facts

WINTER CRAFTS

Table of Contents

Paper Crafts

Wood Crafts

Yarn Crafts

This is the table of contents from a book of winter crafts. Circle parts of the table of contents to answer each question below. Use the colors indicated.

Where would you look to find ...

a craft about trees? (Hint: There is more than one.) *Yellow*

steps for making a sled? *Green*

something you could make with tissue paper? *Blue*

a craft that uses ice pop sticks? *Red*

SKILL: Use text features to locate key facts

ALL ABOUT BRAZIL

Brazil is the biggest country in South America. It has a triangle shape. The capital city is Brasília. The Amazon rainforest is found in Brazil. Brazil touches an ocean. Many of the big cities are near the ocean. One of the longest rivers on Earth is found in Brazil. Most of Brazil is tropical, which means it is hot and gets a lot of rain. Many people in Brazil like soccer. Carnival is a big holiday in Brazil. People celebrate Carnival with parades, costumes, and music. There are many interesting things to see in Brazil.

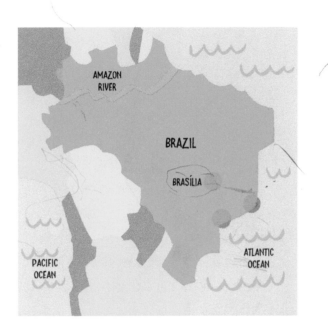

Color the check if the statement is true or the X if the statement is false.

1. Brazil touches the Pacific Ocean. ✓ ✗

2. The Amazon River is in Brazil. ✓ ✗

3. Brasília is next to the ocean. ✓ ✗

4. Brazil is shaped like a triangle. ✓ ✗

SKILL: Use text features to locate key facts

WHAT DOES A CHEMIST DO?

Everything around us is made up of tiny parts called atoms. Chemists work with atoms to make new things. For example, some chemists make medicines, plastics, or cleaning products. They learn about how to combine or take apart elements in different ways. Chemists do tests to see how heat and light change elements. Chemists make healthier dog food, better glue, and brighter paints. Chemists usually work in a science lab. If you like science, you might enjoy being a chemist someday.

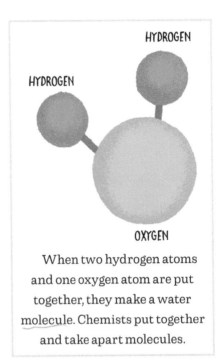

When two hydrogen atoms and one oxygen atom are put together, they make a water molecule. Chemists put together and take apart molecules.

Complete the crossword puzzle.

1. Atoms put together make a _____.

2. Chemists work in a _____ _____. (two words)

3. Chemists make new _____.

4. Chemists test how light and _____ change elements.

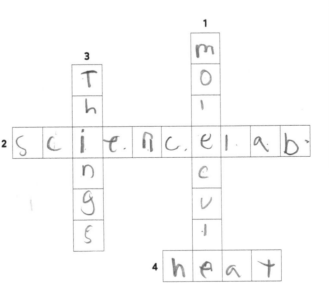

RAINFOREST LAYERS

Rainforests are full of plants and animals that live in the forest's four layers. The lowest layer is the forest floor. It is darkest on the forest floor. Bigger animals like gorillas live here. The next layer up is the understory. Small trees and bushes grow here. Snakes and leopards live in the understory. The next layer up is the canopy. This layer gets lots of sunlight. Monkeys and frogs live here. The tallest trees grow past the canopy and make up the emergent layer. This layer is hot, wet, and windy. Some birds live here. There

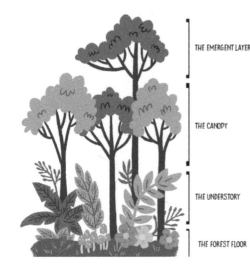

THE EMERGENT LAYER

THE CANOPY

THE UNDERSTORY

THE FOREST FLOOR

are many living things in the rainforest.

Mark the answers in the passage or on the diagram.

1. Draw an arrow to the layer where monkeys (not gorillas) live.

2. Circle the name of the layer that is the darkest.

3. Draw a star next to the highest layer.

SKILL: Explain how images contribute to the text

THE OAK TREE LIFE CYCLE

When you see a big oak tree, it is strange to think that it started out as a tiny seed. If a tree seed lands in soil, it sends down a root and sends up a small sprout. The tiny plant grows little by little. When the plant becomes a tall tree, it can grow flowers. The flowers have yellow dust inside them called pollen. Wind moves the pollen from tree to tree. When a flower gets pollen from a different flower, it can turn into a seed. The seed falls to the ground and the cycle can begin all over again.

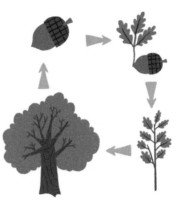

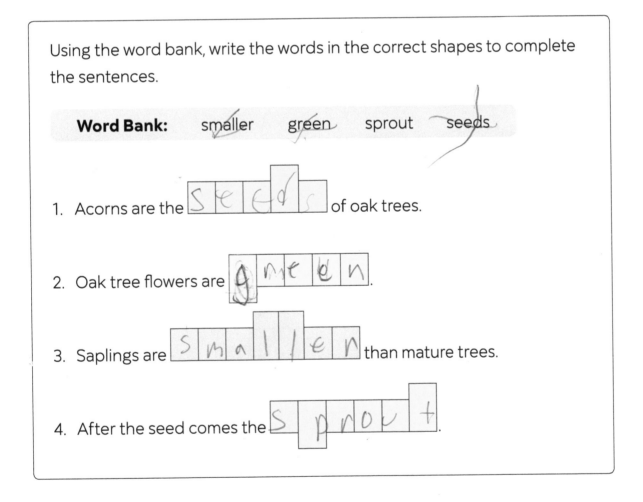

Using the word bank, write the words in the correct shapes to complete the sentences.

Word Bank: smaller green sprout seeds

1. Acorns are the `seeds` of oak trees.

2. Oak tree flowers are `green`.

3. Saplings are `smaller` than mature trees.

4. After the seed comes the `sprout`.

SKILL: Explain how images contribute to the text

HOW TO DRAW A CUBE

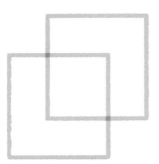 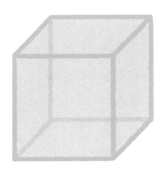 

1. Start by drawing a square. Draw another square that overlaps one of the corners of the first square.

2. Draw diagonal lines to connect the corners between the two squares. Erase the lines that would not be seen through the cube.

3. Finally, add shading to make it look three-dimensional.

Use the text and the pictures above to draw your own cube.

SKILL: Explain how images contribute to the text

HOW MUCH SLEEP DO YOU NEED?

Getting the right amount of sleep helps you think, learn, and create the best you can. Sleep also helps your body grow and heal. As a person gets older, the amount of sleep that they need changes. Babies and young children need a lot of sleep because they are growing and learning new things very quickly. By the time people are adults, they need about eight hours of sleep each night. Adults are not growing anymore and have already learned things like how to talk and walk. How much sleep do you need to be your best self?

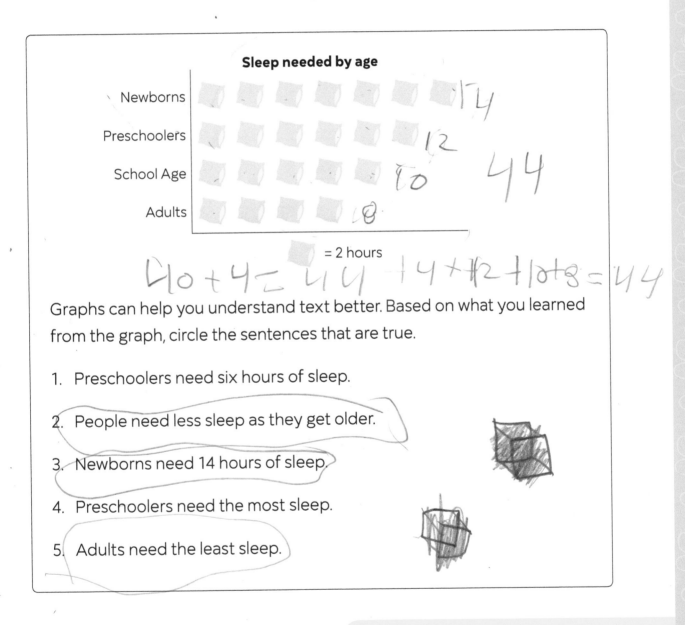

Sleep needed by age

Newborns

Preschoolers

School Age

Adults

□ = 2 hours

Graphs can help you understand text better. Based on what you learned from the graph, circle the sentences that are true.

1. Preschoolers need six hours of sleep.

2. People need less sleep as they get older.

3. Newborns need 14 hours of sleep.

4. Preschoolers need the most sleep.

5. Adults need the least sleep.

SKILL: Explain how images contribute to the text

ALL ABOUT CAVES

Caves are hollow spaces in the crust of the Earth. Sometimes they are made by water that wears away the rock and leaves behind an open space underground. Caves are very dark. Light can only get in if the cave has an opening on the Earth's surface. Animals like bats, rats, and bears take shelter in caves, but they have to leave the cave to find food. A few fish and bugs can live in caves all the time. Dripping water that is full of minerals can make interesting rock shapes inside caves. Caves are very different from aboveground habitats.

Mark on the picture to show how it helps you understand the text.

1. Draw an arrow to the part of the picture that shows the crust of the Earth.

2. Circle the rock shapes formed by dripping water.

3. Draw a star where cave fish might live.

4. Add a plant where it could grow. (Think carefully. Could a plant grow in a cave, or would it have to grow somewhere else?)

SKILL: Explain how images contribute to the text

WHAT CAN TEETH TELL US?

Before you read, it's helpful to think of what you already know about the topic. Then you can connect new information to what you already know. This text is about dinosaur teeth. Using the checklist below, check off anything that you already know or have seen about dinosaurs and teeth.

- [X] I have seen dinosaur bones.
- [✓] I have seen the different shapes of my own teeth.
- [✓] I've heard of plant-eating and meat-eating dinosaurs.

People and dinosaurs did not live at the same time. To learn about dinosaurs, people have to use clues from the dinosaur bones that are left behind. Dinosaur teeth can tell us a lot about how dinosaurs lived. If a dinosaur had sharp teeth, that means it was a meat eater. Sharp, pointy teeth are perfect for tearing into meat. If a dinosaur had flat, rough teeth, that means it was a plant eater. Flat teeth help grind up leaves and grasses. If a dinosaur had some sharp teeth and some flat teeth, that means it ate both meat and plants. Teeth can tell us a lot about dinosaurs.

If you found a dinosaur fossil with flat teeth, what could you guess about that dinosaur?

SKILL: Activate prior knowledge

WORKING DOGS

Think of things that you already know about working dogs. Write them on the chart below. After reading the passage, see if there's anything new you learned that you can add to the chart.

	WORKING DOGS HAVE . . .	WORKING DOGS CAN . . .	WORKING DOGS NEED . . .
Before Reading			

	WORKING DOGS HAVE . . .	WORKING DOGS CAN . . .	WORKING DOGS NEED . . .
After Reading			

Dogs make great pets, but they also have skills that can help people. Some dogs help the police. They can run fast to chase and hold people. They can also smell things that might be unsafe. Search and rescue dogs can find people who are lost. They use their sense of smell to find people. Service dogs can guide people who are blind. Herding dogs can help farmers move animals from one place to another. Working dogs need training to learn how to be helpful. Just like other dogs, they also need love and care from their owners.

SKILL: Activate prior knowledge

HOW CRAYONS ARE MADE

Before reading the passage below, color the check if you think the sentence is true. Color the X if you think the sentence is false. It's OK to guess if you don't know the answer. After reading, use what you learned to mark the sentences again. Did your thinking change?

	BEFORE READING	AFTER READING
1. Crayons are made of paint.	✔ ✗	✔ ✗
2. Heat is needed to make crayons.	✔ ✗	✔ ✗
3. Crayon shapes are cut out with a knife.	✔ ✗	✔ ✗
4. Crayon labels are made of paper.	✔ ✗	✔ ✗

Crayons start as chunks of wax. The wax is heated until it melts into a liquid. Hardening powder and coloring are mixed into the wax. The liquid is poured into crayon-shaped molds. It cools down and becomes hard. The new crayons are taken out of the molds. Next, a paper label is glued on the crayons. The crayons are packed, one of each color, into boxes. Then they are ready to be used for artwork!

SKILL: Activate prior knowledge

THE SECRETS OF SUGAR

Many people love to eat sweet treats like cake, candy, and cookies. Foods that taste sweet have a lot of sugar in them. Sugar is a good source of energy. However, too much sugar is hard on our bodies. If we eat more sugar than our bodies can use, the extra sugar gets stored as fat. Having extra fat makes the heart, bones, and muscles work harder. If sugar stays on your teeth, it can cause cavities. To stay healthy, eat only small amounts of sugary foods and make sure to brush your teeth every day.

Use the tip of a pencil to hold a paper clip loop to the middle of the spinner. Flick the paper clip to spin. Answer the question on the spinner to make connections between your life and the text. Spin several times.

What has a dentist told you about sugar and your teeth?

What have you cooked that has sugar as an ingredient?

Have you ever checked a food label for sugar?

What snacks can you think of that aren't sweet?

ANTARCTICA

If you look at a globe, you will find Antarctica at the very bottom. It is one of Earth's seven continents. Antarctica is very cold and windy. Not much rain or snow falls in Antarctica. It is a frozen desert. When rain or snow falls, it freezes and builds up as ice. It is hard for living things to survive in Antarctica. Trees don't grow in Antarctica. Mosses can be found near the coast. Penguins and seals live in Antarctica. Whales live in the water around Antarctica. The only people that live there are scientists. Antarctica is the harshest of all the continents.

Compare the place you live to Antarctica. Write similarities where the ovals overlap. Write differences in the outside parts of the ovals.

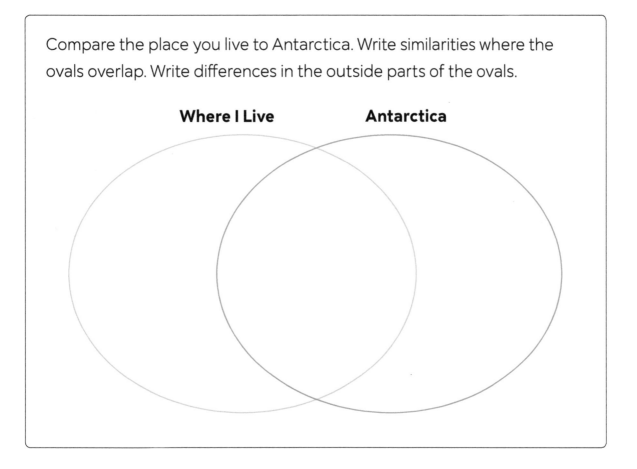

Where I Live   **Antarctica**

SKILL: Make connections to self and the world

THE MISSING BROWNIES

Joey baked brownies and put them on a plate to cool. When he came back to try one, the brownies were all gone! Joey had to find out who took his brownies!

What do you think will happen next? Write your prediction in the space below.

I predict *Joey is going to find his brownis!*

Check your prediction: ✓ ✗

Read the rest of the story below. If your prediction was right, color in the check. If you had to change your thinking, color in the X. It's OK to change your thinking. Good readers do it all the time.

Joey found his dog, Rocky, sleeping on the couch. There weren't any crumbs around him. It wasn't the dog who took Joey's brownies. Joey found his sister, Olivia, playing with dolls in the playroom. It wasn't Olivia who took Joey's brownies. Joey wanted to sit in his treehouse and think about it more.

He opened the back door and found his mom. She was putting out sandwiches, chips, and brownies!

"Surprise!" said Joey's mom. "Let's have a picnic lunch!"

OUR OWN CHRISTMAS

Sonia and her mom always flew to Florida to see the rest of their family for Christmas. One year, a big snowstorm hit Sonia's city. The whole airport was shut down. Sonia's Christmas was ruined!

"We'll have to get groceries," said Sonia's mom. Sonia dragged her feet through the store.

"What should we eat on Christmas?" asked Sonia's mom.

"How about popcorn and cookies?" said Sonia.

Sonia was shocked when her mom said, "OK! We can watch movies."

"Let's play board games, too!" said Sonia.

They missed being with family, but Sonia and her mom found a way to make Christmas fun!

Complete the crossword puzzle.

1. Sonia suggested buying _____ and cookies.
2. What state did Sonia usually visit for Christmas?
3. What kind of weather shut down the airport?
4. What does Sonia suggest they play on Christmas? (two words)
5. At first, Sonia thought Christmas was _____.

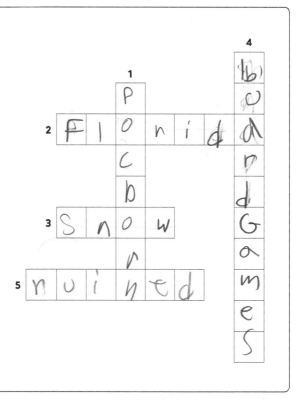

SKILL: Answer questions about key details

WYATT'S PROJECT

Sometimes an author doesn't explain exactly what happened in a story. You have to use what you already know, along with clues the author gives you to figure it out. This is called making an inference. Read each section of the story. Then color the smiley face next to the inference that matches the clues the author gave.

STORY		INFERENCES
Wyatt's grandma had just taught him how to knit. He worked on his knitting on the bus ride to school.	🙂 / 🙂	Wyatt wants to get better at knitting. / Wyatt doesn't like knitting.
"What are you doing?" asked Brandon. "I'm knitting a scarf," said Wyatt. "That's a girl thing to do!" said Brandon. Wyatt just smiled and kept practicing. Each day, his scarf got longer.	🙂 / 🙂	Brandon hurt Wyatt's feelings. / Wyatt doesn't care what Brandon says.
One day, the weather turned windy and cold. Wyatt had finished his knitting project! He wrapped his scarf around his ears and neck. While the other kids were shivering, Wyatt was nice and warm. "Hey, Wyatt," said Brandon, "Do you think you could make me a scarf?"	🙂 / 🙂	Brandon thinks knitting is silly. / Brandon realizes knitting is useful.

SKILL: Answer questions about key details

AN UNLIKELY FRIEND

Belinda the butterfly was following the other butterflies on her first trip south for the winter. Belinda stopped for a short rest. When she opened her eyes again, all the other butterflies were gone!

A goose walked by and said, "Hey, little butterfly. Why are you here by yourself?"

"I was going south for the winter, but now I'm lost!" sobbed Belinda.

"Don't worry," said the goose. "I can help!"

"How do you know about butterfly trips?" asked Belinda.

"Geese go south for the winter, too," explained the goose. He told Belinda which way to go. After a couple of days, she found the other butterflies! Belinda was glad for the help from an unlikely friend.

Color the check if the statement is true or the X if the statement is false.

1. Belinda had flown south many times.

2. Belinda stopped because she was hungry.

3. The goose knew the way.

4. It took Belinda a couple of days to catch up with the other butterflies.

SKILL: Answer questions about key details

THE MUSICIAN AND THE MERMAID ✓

Victor loved to play his guitar. One day he played by the sea and a mermaid appeared.

She said, "Come play music in my underwater home."

Victor jumped into the sea. He played music for the mermaid day after day. Soon, Victor was playing only sad songs.

"I love to play music, but I miss my family," said Victor.

The mermaid also felt sad, thinking of her quiet days under the sea before she heard Victor's music.

"I will take you back, but promise to come play by the sea for me," said the mermaid.

Victor promised. Every day he played his guitar by the sea and the mermaid splashed in the waves.

Mark the text in the passage that answers each question using the color indicated.

1. Who are the characters? *Red*

2. What is the setting? (Hint: There are two of them.) *Blue*

3. Why was Victor sad? *Green*

4. What agreement do Victor and the mermaid come to? *Yellow*

SKILL: Answer questions about key details

RAPUNZEL

√

Once a witch stole a baby named Rapunzel. She locked Rapunzel up in a tall tower. Rapunzel wished she could be free, but the witch would not let her go.

When the witch visited, she yelled, "Rapunzel, let down your hair!" Rapunzel put her long hair out the window and the witch climbed it like a rope. One day, a prince watched this from behind a tree.

After the witch left, he came to the tower and yelled, "Rapunzel, let down your hair!"

He climbed up to the top of the tower. Rapunzel explained that she was a prisoner and wanted to leave. The next day he came back with a rope ladder and they climbed down together. They ran away and lived happily ever after.

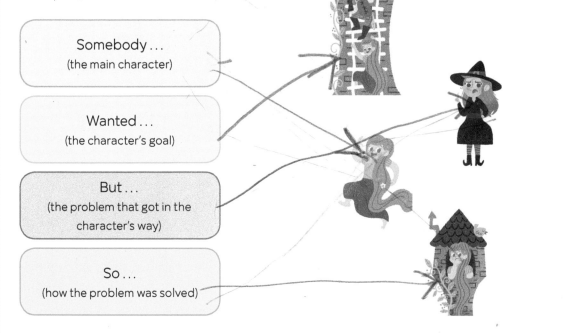

Many stories have a main character who wants something, but an obstacle gets in their way. They find a way to solve the problem in the end. Draw a line to connect each story element with its match from the story above.

Somebody . . .
(the main character)

Wanted . . .
(the character's goal)

But . . .
(the problem that got in the character's way)

So . . .
(how the problem was solved)

SKILL: Retell stories, understanding the central message or lesson

IT'S SO UNFAIR!

Rashad had noticed a few things lately. He had to eat vegetables, but his little sister, Ava, didn't. He had to clean up messes—sometimes ones that he didn't even make. Not his little sister! He always had to share, but Ava was terrible at it. *It is so unfair!* thought Rashad. *When is my dad going to start treating us the same?*

One night, Ava threw a big fit. Rashad's dad put Ava to bed early.

When he came back downstairs, Rashad's dad said, "Little kids need a lot of sleep! We have time to play a video game together if you want."

"Sure!" said Rashad. The rules weren't the same for Rashad and Ava, but sometimes that worked out better for Rashad!

Sometimes characters don't solve their problems by making them stop. Instead, they see the problem in a different way and feel better by the end of the story. This is called a resolution. Like Activity 46, find the "Somebody," "Wanted," "But," and "So" and fill in the blanks with details from the story. This time, "So" has been replaced with "he realizes" to represent a resolution.

__Rashad_____ wanted his dad to treat him and
Somebody – main character

his sister __the same_____. But, when his sister has

to __go to bed_____ early, he realizes that sometimes

different rules __are good_____.

A MIXED-UP PICTURE

Everyone in Vanessa's class was drawing their favorite animal. Vanessa's favorite animal was a cow.

Someone said, "Birds are the best!"

I should really draw a bird, thought Vanessa. She drew wings on her paper.

Someone else said, "Lions are greatest!" Vanessa drew a lion's mane on her paper.

Then someone said, "Fish are cooler than all the other animals!" Vanessa drew a fish tail on her paper.

Then she stopped and realized that she had drawn an animal with wings, a mane, and a fish tail. This was a disaster! Vanessa took a breath and flipped her paper over. She started again with a big body for a cow. She kept going with her own idea until her picture was finished.

Sometimes an author shows how a character changes in a story to teach the reader a lesson. Write a word that makes sense in each blank. Use the shapes to find the letters that complete the last sentence.

Vanessa's favorite animal is a C O W. She hears kids saying that

other a n i m a l s are better. She draws parts from

different animals on her P a p e r. Soon, she sees that her

picture is a d i s a s t e r.

In the end, she learns it is better to stick with

your o w n s d e a.

SKILL: Retell stories, understanding the central message or lesson

A WINDY NIGHT

The howling wind kept Lauren awake. *The wind is so loud*, she thought. *What if it blows the house over?* She felt around her bed for her teddy bear to hug. Suddenly, Lauren realized she left it outside earlier! Lauren put on her jacket, took a deep breath, and pushed the back door open. She saw the bear right where she had left it, tipped over, but not blown away. She stood in the wind for a minute, noticing that it blew her hair around but didn't push her over. Inside, she pulled up her blankets and fell asleep quickly. The wind was loud, but if it couldn't push her over, she knew the big, strong house was just fine.

This story uses character change to help teach a lesson. Draw Lauren at the beginning of the story, and again at the end. Discuss what she learned about the thing she was afraid of.

SKILL: Retell stories, understanding the central message or lesson

NEW NEIGHBORS

A new family moved in next door to Javier. Javier waved to a woman sitting on the porch. The woman didn't wave back. *She's very mean and rude,* thought Javier.

Later, Javier's mom said, "We got some of the new neighbors' mail. Can you take it to them?"

Javier walked to the neighbors' porch and told the woman, "We got some of your mail."

"Thank you!" said the woman. "What's your name?"

"I'm Javier."

The woman said, "I'm Katie. Tell me about the neighborhood. I'm blind so I can't see what it's like."

Javier told her about the big trees, the bus stop, and the duck pond.

After that, when he walked by, Javier said, "Hi, Katie!" instead of waving.

"Hey, Javier!" Katie would answer.

Use the tip of a pencil to hold a paper clip loop to the middle of the spinner. Flick the paper clip to spin. Talk about the part of the story indicated on the spinner. Spin several times.

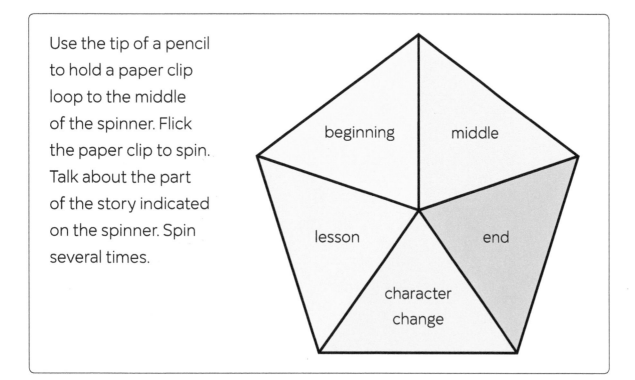

SKILL: Retell stories, understanding the central message or lesson

WHAT'S YOUR PROBLEM?

Sometimes an author shows us the problem in the story through a character's feelings. Draw a line to connect each story to its feeling and problem.

Raul needed to finish his math test, but all he could think about was what was for lunch. His stomach growled.

The character is alone and feels sad.

Jamie looked in her backpack. *Where did I put it?* she wondered. She quickly checked her pockets but didn't pull anything out.

The character is scared because of a strange sound.

Ty sat by himself. He looked over at the kids talking and laughing at the next table. Ty hung his head and sighed.

The character is worried about losing something.

Erin's eyes popped open. She listened hard. *Screech!* There was the sound again! Her heart started racing.

The character feels distracted because of hunger.

SKILL: Describe how characters respond to major events

THE CLEANUP CONTEST

It was a warm day and Owen and his brother, Jesse, were going outside to play basketball.

"Hold on!" said Dad. "Your room is a mess! You're not going out until it's clean."

"Aww, man!" said Owen.

Back in their room, Jesse said, "This is going to take forever!"

Then Owen got an idea. "Let's make it a contest," he said. "Whoever gets their stuff put away the fastest gets the basketball first."

"OK!" said Jesse. He threw clothes in the laundry basket as fast as he could. Owen got to work putting away his toys.

It wasn't long before the brothers were headed back out the door, the basketball in Owen's hands.

Complete each sentence by filling in the word shape.

1. The boys wanted to play `basketball`.

2. The problem was that they had to `clean` their `room` first.

3. Owen turned cleaning into a `contest`.

4. This solution made the work go `fast`.

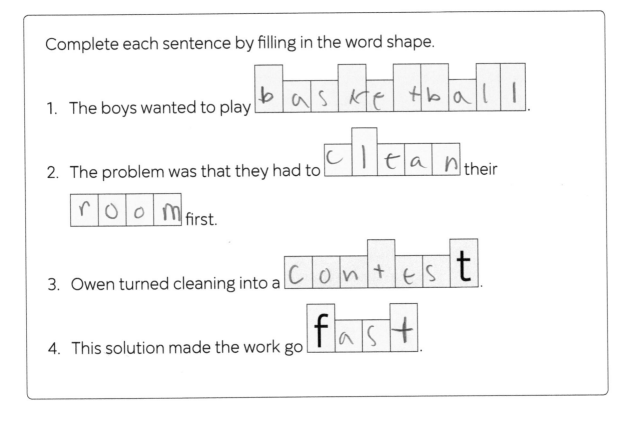

SKILL: Describe how characters respond to major events

TEAM CAPTAIN

Sadie took off her skates after a long practice. She had been working especially hard in practice because her hockey coach would be choosing a team captain soon.

At the next practice, Sadie's coach said, "I've made my decision. This year's team captain will be Jada!" The other girls clapped, but Sadie skated back to the bench.

What do you think Sadie will do next? Write your prediction.

I predict _that Sadie will cry_ Check your prediction:

✓   ✗

_____

_____

As you continue reading, check your prediction. If you were right, color the check. If you had to change your thinking, color the X. It's OK to change your thinking. Good readers do it all the time.

Sadie's coach came over. "I know you wanted to be captain," he said. "It's OK to feel sad. After a while, though, you have to decide if a setback will stop you, or if you will push ahead."

Sadie took a few minutes to calm down. Then she got back on the ice. She loved playing hockey, even if she wasn't the team captain.

SKILL: Describe how characters respond to major events

THE BIGGEST PUMPKIN IN THE PATCH

"This is the one, Mom!" said Feng as he patted the side of a big pumpkin.

"OK. Let's go pay for it," said Feng's mom.

The pumpkin was too heavy for Feng to carry. His mom couldn't help him. She was carrying his baby sister. Other people had wagons to carry their pumpkins. Feng looked around but all of the wagons were being used. He watched another boy easily rolling a wagon with pumpkins in it. That gave him an idea!

Feng turned the pumpkin on its side. He started pushing it. The pumpkin rolled like a wheel. He rolled it all the way to the cashier, then all the way to the car. Feng couldn't wait to carve his jack-o'-lantern at home!

The sentences below state how Feng solves the problem in the story. Each sentence has one word that is wrong. Cross out what is wrong and write in a correction.

> The problem is that Feng's pumpkin is too ~~small~~. *big*

> Feng tries to find a ~~friend~~ to carry it. *Wagon*

> He finds that the wagons are all ~~broken~~. *being used*

> Feng decides to ~~bounce~~ the pumpkin like a wheel. *roll*

SKILL: Describe how characters respond to major events

BUBBLES' ADVENTURE

Bubbles the parrot lived in the city. *Every day is the same*, thought Bubbles. *I eat my birdseed and watch people out the window.*

Bubbles went to visit her cousin, Polly, in the jungle. Surely things would be more exciting there. When Bubbles arrived, it was raining.

"Where do we go to get out of this rain?" Bubbles asked.

"We just get wet," said Polly. "Hey, look out for that snake!" Bubbles flew to another tree. She didn't feel very safe.

The next morning, Bubbles said, "Where's the birdseed? I'm hungry!"

"We have to find bugs to eat," said Polly.

"Ick!" said Bubbles. "I really need to get home."

Back in the city, Bubbles was happy to be dry and safe inside, watching people out the window.

Design a postcard that shows Bubbles on her trip. Include the things that were challenging for her in the jungle. Talk about how Bubbles responded to the challenges.

SKILL: Describe how characters respond to major events

CHIPMUNK'S LULLABY

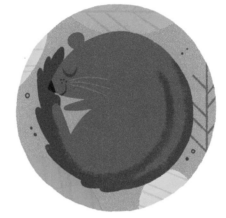

When leaves have fallen on the ground,
And cold wind stirs them all around,
Inside the trees, the chipmunks pile
Seeds and nuts to last a while.

Blades of grass they hide away,
Preparing for a comfy stay,
Making beds both soft and warm,
A shelter from the winter storm.

Underneath a cloud-filled sky,
Downy flakes of snow will fly.
While in their burrows dark and deep,
Curled up tight, the chipmunks sleep.

Poets sometimes use rhyming words to give their poems
a rhythm or beat.

Circle each pair of rhyming words. For example, draw a circle
that encloses the words "ground" and "around" together.

The rhythm in this poem is gentle. Talk about why the poet
would use a gentle rhythm for this topic.

SKILL: Describe how words and phrases give
rhythm and meaning to stories and poems

COOL CLANGING IN THE KITCHEN

On a regular Wednesday,
Pedro plops down his pot.
His pitter-pattering palms
Lay down the beat.
My fork flips and flashes,
Splashes of sound.
Making metallic music,
A kitchen-band of two.
Sal slides in.
His spoons slip and slap,
His toes tip and tap.
Now it's three-o, a trio,
Soon Dad wants to know,
What's all this cool clanging in the kitchen?

Sometimes poets use words with the same beginning sound near each other. For example: Pedro plops down his pot. This is called **alliteration**. Alliteration creates an interesting sound in poems.

Count how many times the letter P is used for alliteration in the poem. Mark the words if it helps you count. Next, color a square on the graph for each word that you counted. Repeat with the letters S, F, and M.

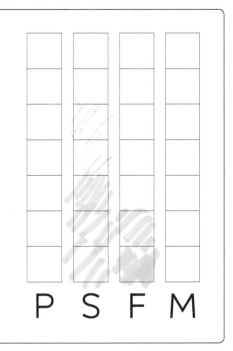

P S F M

SKILL: Describe how words and phrases give rhythm and meaning to stories and poems

A BUSY ANT

The ant woke at sunrise.
Today he would build a tunnel.
No one else was awake,
But the ant started digging.
Soon, a snail slid by,
Rubbing sleep from his eyes.
"I savor slow sunrises," he said.
The ant kept digging.

Later, a bird landed lightly,
And stretched her wings.
"I'm off to snooze in the shade," she said.
The ant kept digging.

A beetle skittered through,
Playing chase with a friend.
"You'll never catch me!" he shouted.
The ant kept digging.

Clouds blew in on the breeze,
Raindrops started falling.
The ant crawled in his new tunnel.
He was done digging.

Sometimes poets repeat something to show that it is important or ongoing. Underline the repeated line in this poem. Think about what the repeated line tells us about the ant. Then mark your answers below by coloring the check if the statement is true or the X if it is false.

1. The ant takes a lot of breaks.

   ✓   ✗

2. Building the tunnel takes a while.

       ✗

3. The ant is a hardworking character.

   ✓   ✗

4. The ant's work paid off in the end.

       ✗

SKILL: Describe how words and phrases give rhythm and meaning to stories and poems

ASTRONAUT BLASTS OFF

Sitting ready in the shuttle,
Strapped in snugly with a buckle.
Close the hatch and seal it tightly,
Buttons light the capsule brightly.
Ground crew members feeling eager,
Call the countdown through the speaker.

Five gloved fingers work together,
Four big windows show great weather,
Three strong engines holding steady,
Two hands hold on, scared but ready,
One big breath in heavy gear,
Blast off past Earth's atmosphere!

Circle the rhyming words in green.

Underline examples of alliteration (where
the author uses words with the same
beginning sound close to each other) in blue.

Notice the repeated use of number words. What does this have to do
with a space shuttle launch?

SKILL: Describe how words and phrases give
rhythm and meaning to stories and poems

FEEL THE BEAT

Some poems have a regular, steady beat that you can tap your food to. Others do not.

Revisit the poems below. Check if the beat is regular or not (irregular). Then put a check next to the feelings that match the rhythm and words in the poem.

From "Chipmunk's Lullaby"

Underneath a cloud-filled sky,
Downy flakes of snow will fly.
While in their burrows dark and deep,
Curled up tight, the chipmunks sleep.

Rhythm:
☑ Regular ☐ Irregular
The Poem Feels:
☑ Gentle ☐ Nervous
☐ Energetic ☐ Sad
☐ Playful ☐ Surprising

From "Cool Clanging in the Kitchen"

My fork flips and flashes,
Splashes of sound.
Making metallic music,
A kitchen-band of two.

Rhythm:
☐ Regular ☐ Irregular
The Poem Feels:
☐ Gentle ☐ Nervous
☐ Energetic ☐ Sad
☑ Playful ☐ Surprising

From "Astronaut Blasts Off"

Five gloved fingers work together,
Four big windows show great weather,
Three strong engines holding steady,
Two hands hold on, scared but ready,
One big breath in heavy gear,
Blast off past Earth's atmosphere!

Rhythm:
☐ Regular ☑ Irregular
The Poem Feels:
☐ Gentle ☐ Nervous
☑ Energetic ☐ Sad
☐ Playful ☐ Surprising

SKILL: Describe how words and phrases give rhythm and meaning to stories and poems

GOLDILOCKS AND THE THREE BEARS

One day, Goldilocks was walking in the woods. She found an empty cottage and decided to go inside. Goldilocks found three chairs and tried each of them. She accidentally broke the smallest one! Goldilocks ate some porridge left on the table and then felt tired. She lay on each of the three beds. The littlest bed was just right for her, so she fell asleep.

Soon, the bears that lived in the cottage returned from a walk. They noticed the broken chair and the empty bowl on the table. Baby Bear shouted, "Mom! Dad! Come look at what's in my bed!" Goldilocks woke up to three angry bear faces staring at her. She screamed and ran away, never to return.

Since this is a familiar story that you may have heard before, pretend that you're the teacher. Use the tip of a pencil to hold a paper clip loop to the middle of the spinner. Flick the paper clip to spin. Use the word on the spinner to make a question about the story. See if someone else can answer your question. Spin several times.

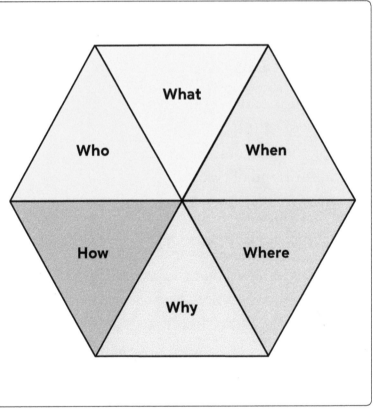

SKILL: Answer questions about key details

GOLDILOCKS AND THE THREE SLOTHS

A family of sloths left their hut for a slow stroll in the jungle. While they were gone, a girl named Goldilocks found their hut and went inside. She sat down at the table and helped herself to a mango. Suddenly, the chair broke beneath her! It was made for sloths, not for girls. Goldilocks noticed some hammocks hanging in the hut. She climbed in and out of each one until she found a small one that was comfortable. Goldilocks had a long nap and then left the hut.

At the end of the day, the sloth family returned.

"What happened to my chair?" asked Baby Sloth. "And who ate my mango?"

To this day, the sloths have no idea what happened in their hut while they were away.

Compare "Goldilocks and the Three Sloths" with "Goldilocks and the Three Bears." Write similarities where the ovals overlap and differences in the outer parts of the ovals.

Goldilocks and the Three Bears

Goldilocks and the Three Sloths

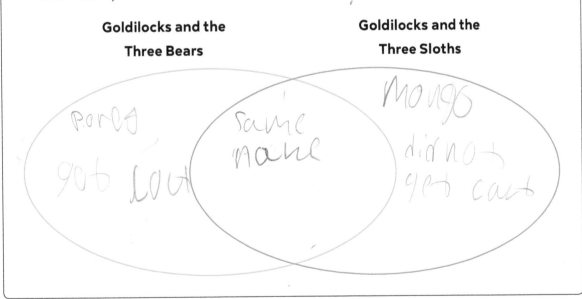

poreg got cold

same name

mongo did not get cold

SKILL: Compare two versions of the same story

THE GINGERBREAD MAN

An old woman baked a gingerbread man. He came to life and ran away across the farm. He ran past the sheep and around the pigs. Soon he came to a river.

"I'll give you a ride across," said a fox. The gingerbread man jumped on his tail. A moment later, the fox flipped the gingerbread man and caught him in his mouth. That was the end of the gingerbread man.

In a city apartment, a woman pulled a gingerbread man out of the oven. He popped off the pan and ran away! The gingerbread man waved to some kids in the hallway and then ran down the stairs. He stopped in front of a busy street.

"I can help you cross," said a girl. But as soon as she picked him up, *chomp*! That was the end of the gingerbread man.

Compare the two versions of "The Gingerbread Man." Draw an arrow on each dial to show if the parts of the two stories are exactly the same, totally different, or somewhere in between. Talk about why you drew each arrow the way you did.

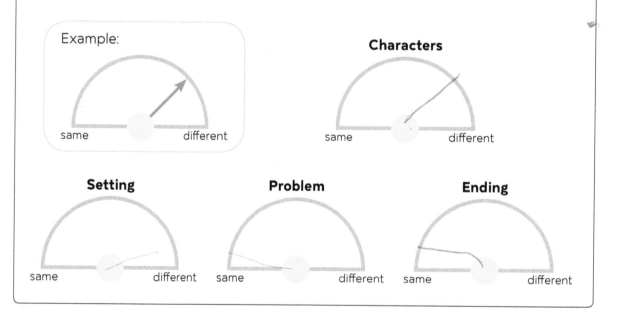

SKILL: Compare two versions of the same story

HOW THE SPIDER GOT THIN LEGS

Anansi the spider visited a friend who was cooking. To get out of helping, Anansi tied a web from one of his legs to his friend's pan.

"When it's ready," said Anansi, "pull the web and I'll come have some." Anansi did the same thing at other friends' houses until a web was tied to each of his legs. Soon, all the strings were pulling Anansi's legs at the same time. This is how spiders got long, thin legs.

It was dinnertime and Anansi was stirring a pot of food for his friend.

He heard another friend yell, "Anansi, I know you have many legs. Stretch so you can help stir my pot, too." Others saw what was happening and they also asked for help cooking. Soon, Anansi's legs were stretched long and thin in eight different directions.

Write a word that makes sense in each blank to compare the two stories. Use the shapes to find the letters that complete the last sentence.

The main character in both stories is ___ ___ ___ ___ ___ ___. In the
▲

first story, he is greedy. He wants to eat everyone's ___ ___ ___ ___ but
●

get out of ___ ___ ___ ___ ___ ___ ___. In the second version, Anansi
▲

helps ___ t ___ ___ many pots. In both stories Anansi's legs
■

get ___ t ___ ___ ___ ___ ___ ___ ___ ___.
⬟

The original Anansi story is from ___ ___ ___ ___ ___ ___.
▲ ● ■ ⬥ ⬟ ▲

SKILL: Compare two versions of the same story

BUG-EATING PLANTS

Most plants need soil, water, and sunlight to survive. Venus flytraps are different. They also need to catch insects to live and grow. Plants need something called nitrogen. Other plants get nitrogen from the soil they live in. Venus flytraps grow in soil that has very little nitrogen. Instead, they get nitrogen from insects.

Venus flytraps have special leaves that look like jaws with sharp teeth. On the inside of the leaves are tiny hairs. If an insect touches these hairs, the "jaws" of the Venus flytrap snap shut! Then the plant covers the insect in liquid that breaks it down. This allows the Venus flytrap to get the insect's nitrogen.

Write at least one detail from the text in each section of the chart below.

VENUS FLYTRAPS NEED . . .	VENUS FLYTRAPS CAN . . .	VENUS FLYTRAPS HAVE . . .

PYRAMIDS IN EGYPT

Long ago, near the Nile River in Egypt, many pyramids were built. The largest pyramid probably took about 20 years to build. Workers had to cut, move, and stack heavy blocks of stone. Inside the pyramids, they made rooms and walkways. The walls of the rooms were decorated with paintings. The pyramids were built as a place to bury Egyptian kings. Egyptians buried their kings with food, jewels, weapons, and clothing. They believed the kings would need these things when they lived on in the afterlife. Many people go to see the pyramids, which are still standing today.

Use details from the passage to draw what might be in one of the rooms inside a pyramid.

SKILL: Ask and answer questions about key details

SHELTER ON THE GREAT PLAINS

Long ago, some Native Americans lived in tipis. A tipi is a kind of tent that is shaped like a cone. It is made from animal skins on wooden poles. People who lived in tipis could build a fire inside for warmth and let the smoke out the smoke flaps at the top. Eight to 10 people could live in a tipi.

Tipis were used by Native Americans who lived on flat land called the Great Plains. They needed to be able to move their homes so they could follow the animals that they hunted. Tipis can be taken down, moved, and set up again somewhere else. They were a useful, portable shelter.

Each sentence below has one word that is wrong. Cross out what is wrong and write in a correction.

1. All Native Americans built tipis.

2. Tipis are made from metal poles and animal skins.

3. The hole at the top of a tipi lets out birds.

4. Tipis are built to be permanent.

SKILL: Ask and answer questions about key details

WORKING IN A DENTAL OFFICE

It takes many different kinds of workers to keep a dental office running. At the front desk are the office staff members. These people make appointments, collect payments, and keep track of records. Office staff members need to be organized and friendly.

Other people in a dental office work with teeth. A dental hygienist is the person who cleans your teeth. They also teach people how to take care of their teeth. The dentist fixes problems with teeth. Dentists fill cavities, pull teeth, and fix broken teeth. A dental assistant cleans dental tools, takes x-rays, and helps the dentist fix teeth. Do you think you might enjoy working in a dental office someday?

Read the passage to someone. Then think of questions about the text that start with the words below. Color in a star for each kind of question the other person can answer. See how many stars the other person can get!

Who   **What**   **Which**

SKILL: Ask and answer questions about key details

LIFE ON THE ICE

Polar bears live in the Arctic near ocean shores. They survive by eating seals. In the coldest months, ice forms over parts of the ocean. Polar bears leave the land and go out onto the ice to hunt. The bears wait by a hole in the ice. When a seal comes to the hole for air, the polar bear can catch it. Polar bears can also swim under the ice for hunting.

Temperatures on Earth have started getting warmer over the past few decades. Warmer weather makes the ice melt earlier. It is difficult for polar bears to survive with temperatures getting warmer. They depend on their icy habitat for hunting.

Complete the crossword puzzle using words from the passage above.

1. What polar bears eat.

2. Ice forms on the ocean in the _____ months.

3. Temperatures on Earth are getting _____.

4. Ice has started to melt _____.

5. Polar bears need ice for _____.

SKILL: Ask and answer questions about key details

WHICH TITLE WORKS?

In this activity, you'll choose the title that best matches all of the paragraphs. Draw a line to match each paragraph to its topic.

The biggest land animal is the elephant. They grow about as tall as two humans stacked on top of each other. Blue whales are much bigger. They are about as long as half a football field.

Speed Records

Africa is home to many animals that can run fast. Cheetahs are the fastest animal. They can run as fast as cars on the highway. Antelopes are just a little slower than cheetahs.

Life-span Records

Some animals can live much longer than people. There are tortoises that can live longer than 150 years. Bowhead whales can also have long lives. The oldest one lived to be 211 years old.

Size Records

Think about what all three paragraphs have in common. Circle the title below that best fits the topics of all three paragraphs.

How to Find Animals   **All About Fast Animals**

Animal Record Setters   **Animals of Africa**

SKILL: Identify the main topic of multi-paragraph texts

TOPIC MIX-UP

1. Many machines like cars, lawnmowers, and planes burn gasoline for energy. Gasoline starts out as oil. Oil is a liquid that forms underground from plants and animals that died long ago. Oil is turned into gasoline at a factory.

2. Have you ever seen flat black panels on top of houses? These are solar panels. They take in sunlight and turn it into electricity. This electricity is used to make things like heaters and dishwashers in the home run.

3. If you've seen a wind turbine, you've seen wind power being collected. Wind turbines are held up on a strong pole. They have three long blades that spin. The wind turns the blades and makes electricity.

In the three smaller spaces, write the topic that matches each paragraph. Then write the topic that fits all three of the paragraphs in the large space at the top. Not all topic choices will be used.

Topic Choices:

Energy from Oil   Energy from Food

Where Energy Comes From   Wind Energy

Energy from the Sun   The Best Kind of Power

SKILL: Identify the main topic of multi-paragraph texts

WORLD'S BIGGEST PRIMATES

1. Gorillas have a lot of variety in their diets. They eat plant material such as leaves, stems, fruits, and flowers. Gorillas also eat meat in small amounts. They will eat snails and insects.

2. Gorillas do not live alone. They are found in family groups. A group of gorillas is called a troop. They eat, sleep, and play together. Gorillas in troops bond by cleaning each other's fur.

3. Gorillas have large, heavy bodies. They are bigger than other apes and monkeys. Gorillas are usually seen walking on their feet and hands. Some of the larger males grow gray fur on their backs. They are called silverbacks.

For each topic below, circle the paragraph number that contains the information. Hint: One of the topics below can be found in all three paragraphs.

How gorillas look	1	2	3
Facts about gorillas	1	2	3
Gorillas' social lives	1	2	3
What gorillas eat	1	2	3

Note: The topic that can be found in all three paragraphs is also the topic of the whole text.

SKILL: Identify the main topic of multi-paragraph texts

IT TAKES MORE THAN PILOTS

Airports are busy places where people do many different jobs. Air traffic controllers keep planes moving in and out of the airport safely. They talk to pilots on radios and let them know when to land or take off. Air traffic controllers work in tall towers with windows so they can see the planes all around them.

Airports also have security workers. These people use x-ray scanners and metal detectors. They check people and baggage to make sure nothing dangerous is brought on a plane.

Mechanics also work at airports. They solve problems and make sure planes are running correctly. Airplane mechanics have to know a lot about how airplanes work. These people and many others make air travel possible.

Mark your answers below by coloring the check if the statement is true or the X if it is false.

1. The topic of paragraph one is airplane pilots.

2. Paragraph two is all about airport security workers.

3. The topic of paragraph three is car mechanics.

4. The topic of the whole passage is jobs at airports.

SKILL: Identify the main topic of multi-paragraph texts

SHARK SENSES

Sharks are **cunning** hunters. Their senses help them catch their **prey**. Sharks can see in dark or **murky** water because they have excellent eyesight. Sharks can also sense electricity. When an animal **contracts** its muscles, a little bit of electricity is made. This electricity tells sharks that animals are moving nearby. The best way to be safe from a shark is to be far away.

Glossary

contracts – squeezes or tightens

cunning – good at tricking

murky – cloudy or unclear

prey – animal that is killed for food

The glossary explains the meaning of the bold words in the text. Use the text and the glossary to write a word that makes sense in each blank. Use the shapes to find the letters that complete the last sentence.

Even in water that is murky and ___ ___ ___ ___ ,

sharks can still hunt their ___ ___ ___ ___.

Sharks can sense ___ ___ ___ ___ ___ ___ ___ ___ ___ ___ ___

when an animal ___ ___ ___ ___ ___ ___ ___ ___ ___ its muscles.

A shark's skin feels like ___ ___ ___ ___ ___ ___ ___ ___ ___ ___.

SKILL: Use text features to locate key facts

IMPORTANT INVENTIONS

Index

compass, 6

computer

   laptop, 17

   personal, 14

engines

   internal combustion, 12, 13

   steam, 11

paper, 7

Watt, James, 11

wheel, 5

Notice:

- Some topics can be found on more than one page.
- People's names are listed with the last name first.
- Subentries show different types of something (like with "engines").

Indexes are found at the back of some books. They show which pages contain information on specific topics. Answer each question below by writing in the correct page number. If the math problems are correct, your answers are right!

Where would you look to find out when the wheel was invented?

What page has information about laptop computers?

What page would tell you about the invention of paper?

$+$

Which page would tell you about James Watt?

$-$

Where is the first page on internal combustion engines?

Where could you find out what a compass is?

SKILL: Use text features to locate key facts

RECREATION WEBSITE

Blue Springs
Recreation

🔍

Parks	Swimming Pool	Sports ▾	Summer Camp

T-Ball

Spring T-ball leagues are forming now! Teams practice and play starting the first Saturday in April. Players must be three to five years old. To sign up, click <u>HERE</u>.

| Basketball |
| Baseball |
| Flag Football |
| Soccer |
| Volleyball |

On a website, you can click words and pictures to get to other pages. Circle the words or pictures on the website in the colors indicated to show where you would click to do the following:

Search the website for something you don't see on this page *Yellow*

Find out about flag football *Blue*

Find out when the pool is open *Red*

Sign up for T-ball *Green*

SKILL: Use text features to locate key facts

BIKES THEN AND NOW

Bicycles have changed a lot over time. The first bicycle was made in 1817. It was called the running machine because the rider pushed it along with their feet. Pedals were added to bicycles around 1840. In 1871, a style of bicycle called the ordinary was built. It had a large wheel in front and a small wheel in the back. In 1885, the safety bicycle design came out. It had gears and rubber tires. Around 1970, stunt riding on BMX bikes became popular.

Long Ago   **Today**

1817	1871	1885	1970
Running Machine	Ordinary Bicycle	Safety Bicycle	BMX Bicycle

Mark on the time line according to these directions:

1. Draw a dot and write the current year on the far-right side of the time line.
2. Circle the oldest kind of bike on the time line.
3. Draw a box around the kind of bike that came after the ordinary bike.
4. In 1981, after the BMX bike, the mountain bike was made. Add a dot and "MB" to the time line.

SKILL: Use text features to locate key facts

THE GREAT WALL OF CHINA

Construction of the Great Wall

Long ago, the Great Wall of China was built to keep out enemies. At first, the wall was made by pressing dirt and gravel down into wood frames. Later, workers used bricks and stone to make the wall stronger. Over the years, many parts of the Great Wall have crumbled. Some of it has been rebuilt.

A Must-See in China

One of the most popular sights to see in China is the Great Wall. People usually go to parts of the wall that are near cities. Visitors can walk along parts of the wall that have been rebuilt. The best time to visit the Great Wall is in spring or fall when the weather is not too hot or too cold.

For each passage, check off the things you noticed. Talk about what was the same in both passages and what was different.

	Construction of the Great Wall	A Must-See in China
MAIN TOPIC	☐ The Great Wall of China ☐ Bricks	☐ The Great Wall of China ☐ Bricks
FACTS	☐ What the wall is made of ☐ What the wall is like today ☐ What the wall was like long ago ☐ When to visit the Great Wall ☐ What you can do at the Great Wall ☐ The rebuilding of the wall	☐ What the wall is made of ☐ What the wall is like today ☐ What the wall was like long ago ☐ When to visit the Great Wall ☐ What you can do at the Great Wall ☐ The rebuilding of the wall

SKILL: Compare important points in two texts on the same topic

HONEYBEES

How Bees Make Honey

Bees collect a liquid called nectar from flowers. They keep the nectar in their special honey stomach. Here, the nectar starts breaking down into sugars. Back at the hive, bees put the liquid in the honeycomb. They fan their wings to dry it out a little bit. Then they put a wax cap on the honeycomb and the honey is finished.

Disappearing Bees

Bees live in hives with many other bees. Sometimes, all the worker bees will suddenly leave a hive. No one knows for sure why this happens. Bees are important because, as they collect nectar, they spread pollen from plant to plant. The spread of pollen helps fruits and seeds form. Scientists are trying to learn how to keep beehives healthy.

Color-code the two passages according to the directions below.

Circle the topic in each passage every time it is mentioned. *Red*

Underline something that is mentioned in both passages. Mark it in both passages. *Green*

Underline a fact in each passage that is unique (not mentioned in the other passage). *Blue*

SKILL: Compare important points in two texts on the same topic

PLACES FOR PIGS

A Different Kind of Pet

Most people think of pigs as farm animals, but some people keep pigs as pets. Potbellied pigs are popular pets because they are smaller than other pigs. Potbellied pigs live inside but need time to play outside. They can be trained to use a litter box. Some people even train their potbellied pigs to do simple tricks.

Pig Farming

Pigs on farms are raised for their meat. Farmers have to help pigs stay cool because pigs do not sweat. Some pigs wallow in mud to stay cool, and some farmers use water misters to keep pigs cool. Pigs also need hay for bedding, clean water, and a diet of pig feed and vegetables.

Write facts that both passages have in common where the ovals overlap. Write something unique about each passage in the outside parts of the ovals.

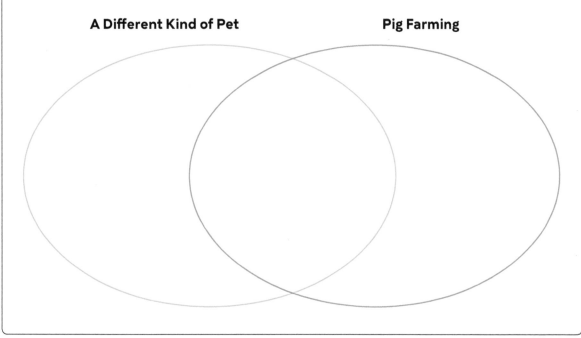

A Different Kind of Pet   Pig Farming

SKILL: Compare important points in two texts on the same topic

MUFFIN SURPRISE

Will liked cooking without recipes. A lot of the time, he ended up with something slimy in a bowl. Will's mom followed recipes exactly as they were written. One day, Will's mom was making blueberry muffins.

"Oh, no!" she said. "I need to go to the store for more blueberries." When she left, Will thought of a surprise for her. He sliced strawberries and added them to the batter. Then he put the batter in the muffin pan and asked his dad to help him put the pan in the oven, not sure how they would turn out.

"What's that delicious smell?" asked Will's mom when she got home.

"Surprise!" said Will. "I finished the muffins with strawberries instead of blueberries."

Will and his mom enjoyed the muffins that they both helped make.

Each sentence below has one word that is wrong. Cross out what is wrong and write in a correction.

1. Will always used recipes when cooking.

2. Will added nuts to the muffin batter.

3. The muffins smelled disgusting.

4. Will's mom hated the muffins.

SKILL: Ask and answer questions about key details

MORNING RUSH

Jaylene sat up suddenly in bed. The sun was already bright in the sky. Her dad must have forgotten to wake her up. She had to get ready quickly so she wouldn't miss the bus. Jaylene got dressed and combed her hair. She grabbed her backpack and a granola bar to eat on the ride.

She opened the front door and looked across the street. Nobody else was at the bus stop. Maybe she was too late! Just then, her friend Elena came by, walking her dog.

"What's going on?" asked Jaylene. "You can't take your dog on the bus."

"I'm not getting on the bus, silly," said Elena. "It's Saturday!" Jaylene and Elena had a good laugh.

Complete the sentences by filling in the word shapes.

⬚⬚⬚⬚⬚⬚⬚ wants to get to the ⬚⬚ on time.

The problem is, she woke up ⬚⬚⬚⬚. Outside, there is

⬚⬚⬚⬚⬚ at the bus stop. She realizes that she doesn't

have school because it's ⬚⬚⬚⬚⬚.

THE MUDDY PUPPY

Ace was a puppy at an animal shelter. Every day when the dogs went outside, Ace ran straight for the mud. One day a family came to the shelter to pick out a puppy. When the mom got to Ace, she pulled her hand back.

"This little guy is cute, but he's such a mess!" she said. The family took home a different puppy. The next day, instead of playing in the mud, Ace splashed in the water bowl outside. Then he lay in the sun to dry. Later, a man came in, looking for a puppy. He fell in love with Ace's soft fur and adopted him. Ace still loved mud, but he realized sometimes it was a good idea to clean up.

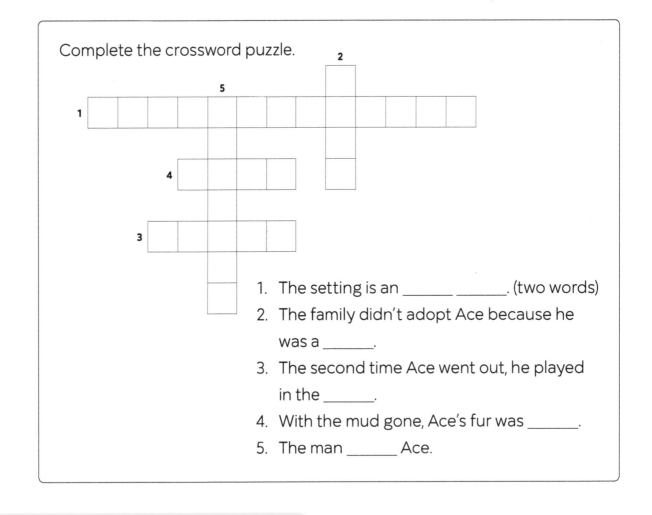

Complete the crossword puzzle.

1. The setting is an _____ _____. (two words)
2. The family didn't adopt Ace because he was a _____.
3. The second time Ace went out, he played in the _____.
4. With the mud gone, Ace's fur was _____.
5. The man _____ Ace.

CAMELS DON'T SWIM

Dax was a camel who lived at the zoo. He watched the seals swimming and thought it looked like fun. His friend Millie saw him looking at the seals one day.

"Give it up!" said Millie. "Camels don't swim." Later that night, when all the visitors had left, Dax unlatched his pen and went out. He gathered up all the seat cushions from the zoo's food court. He tied the cushions together into a raft and threw it into the seals' water tank. Then, with a brave leap, Dax jumped onto the raft.

"Look at Dax!" said Millie. All the other camels watched as Dax paddled around with the seals.

Have someone else read the text. Then write questions that would lead them to get the correct answers below.

The answer is seat cushions. What is the question?

_____

_____

_____

The answer is Millie. What is the question?

_____

_____

_____

SKILL: Ask and answer questions about key details

SUMMER STORIES

It was a new school year and the kids in Nate's class were writing about what they did over the summer. Some kids had been on amazing trips. Nate had just stayed home. He hoped his writing would be interesting, even though he hadn't gone anywhere.

At sharing time, Nate read his story to the class. He wrote about living in a castle, fighting dragons, and looking for gold.

At the end, Cody raised his hand and said, "That was a great story, but it can't be real." Nate explained that he built a blanket fort and wrote about all of his imaginary adventures.

The class clapped! They couldn't wait to hear what Nate would write next.

Using the colors indicated, underline the words or phrases that match the "Somebody," "Wanted," "But," and "So" parts of the story (see Activity 46).

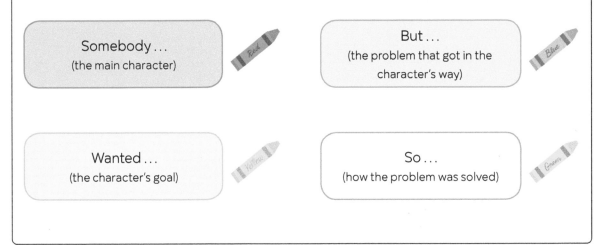

Somebody...
(the main character)
Red

But...
(the problem that got in the character's way)
Blue

Wanted...
(the character's goal)
Yellow

So...
(how the problem was solved)
Green

SKILL: Retell stories, understanding the central message or lesson

ASHLEY AND THE TRAINS

Ashley got very excited and loud when she played with trains.

"OH, NO! The train is going to crash!" she would yell. One day, Ashley's brother was trying to study.

"WHOA! It's a steep hill!" yelled Ashley. Her mom came around the corner.

"If you don't stop yelling, I'll have to put your trains away. Your brother needs it quiet," said her mom.

Ashley could feel the excitement building as she pushed her train to the big hill. The train zoomed down. Ashley threw her hands up and shook them in silent celebration.

She whispered, "Yes!" Ashley crashed a couple of trains together and stood up to turn in silent circles. Her mom came in later.

"I thought maybe you fell asleep," said her mom. "It's been so quiet in here."

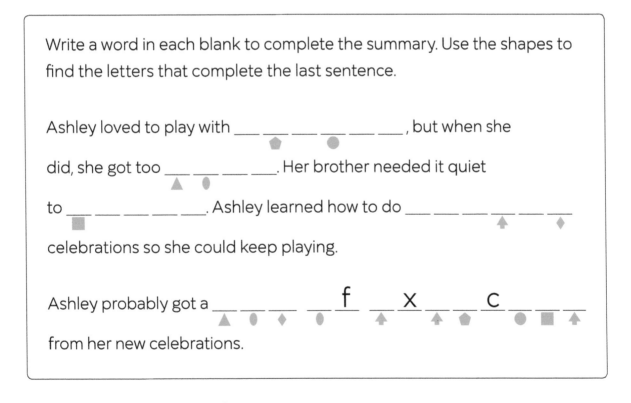

Write a word in each blank to complete the summary. Use the shapes to find the letters that complete the last sentence.

Ashley loved to play with ___ ___ ___ ___ ___ ___ , but when she did, she got too ___ ___ ___ ___. Her brother needed it quiet to ___ ___ ___ ___ ___. Ashley learned how to do ___ ___ ___ ___ ___ ___ celebrations so she could keep playing.

Ashley probably got a ___ ___ ___ ___ f ___ x ___ c ___ ___ ___ from her new celebrations.

SKILL: Retell stories, understanding the central message or lesson

TYLER'S PLAY

Tyler broke his leg by slipping on ice. He would have to take a few weeks off from playing with his basketball team, and they had just started learning plays.

One day, Tyler sat on his bed with a basket of toys. He pulled out some action figures and a bouncy ball. Tyler set up the toys as a basketball team on his bedspread. He moved the ball and the players, acting out a game.

Even though Tyler couldn't play, he went to the next practice.

"Hey, Coach!" said Tyler. "I have an idea for a new play." The coach let Tyler explain the play to the team.

"Great thinking, Tyler!" said the coach. "How did you come up with such a clever play?" Tyler smiled.

Use words or pictures to complete the "Somebody," "Wanted," "But," and "So" parts of the story. Can you retell the four parts you identified? Talk about what lesson we can learn from Tyler.

Somebody . . . (the main character)	Wanted . . . (the character's goal)	But . . . (the problem that got in the character's way)	So . . . (how the problem was solved)

SKILL: Retell stories, understanding the central message or lesson

THE CROW AND THE PITCHER

It had been very dry and Crow was thirsty. He found a pitcher of water that was tall and had a narrow neck. The pitcher was half full with water, but Crow could not get his beak far enough into the pitcher to get it. Crow sat down, certain that he would die of thirst. The sun shone down on him as he stared at the pebbles by his feet. Then he got an idea. Crow picked up one pebble at a time and put them in the pitcher. As the pebbles started to take up space in the bottom of the pitcher, the water was pushed higher and higher. Soon, the water was high enough that Crow could have a delicious drink.

Read the sentences below. Color the check if the sentence is true or the X if it is false.

1. Crow wanted to drink some water because it was hot and dry. ✓ ✗

2. The problem was that the pitcher was empty. ✓ ✗

3. Crow put pebbles in the pitcher to make it heavier. ✓ ✗

4. The lesson is that sometimes you have to get creative to solve a problem. ✓ ✗

SKILL: Retell stories, understanding the central message or lesson

MEGAN'S EARS

One morning Megan looked in the mirror and saw that she had grown mouse ears! She had to give a presentation at school about Amelia Earhart, the famous pilot. Megan was embarrassed to stand in front of people!

The school day started and Mrs. Wendell didn't see Megan in her seat.

"Who wants to give their presentation first?" asked Mrs. Wendell.

"I'll go first!" said a voice at the door. It was Megan. She was dressed up like Amelia Earhart. No one else had thought of dressing up. She had tucked her ears into her hat. Megan wore the costume all day.

When she woke up the next day, Megan's ears were magically back to normal.

Sometimes characters face a problem in the world around them (an external problem) and a problem inside of themselves (an internal problem). When this happens, they have to come up with a solution. Draw lines to connect each part of the story to its label.

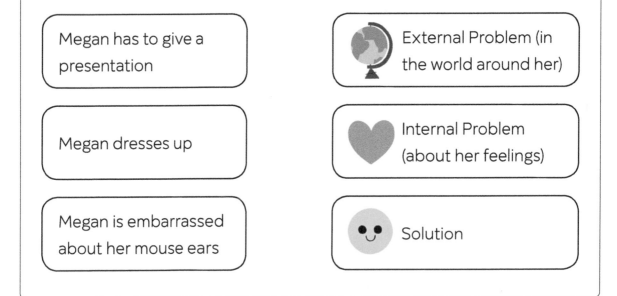

Megan has to give a presentation		External Problem (in the world around her)
Megan dresses up		Internal Problem (about her feelings)
Megan is embarrassed about her mouse ears		Solution

SKILL: Describe how characters respond to major events

TURKEY FOR LUNCH

Ginger ran a school cafeteria. She had planned a turkey lunch to serve the kids before Thanksgiving. The day of the special meal, Ginger realized the turkey had not been delivered. She wouldn't be able to make the turkey lunch that the kids had been looking forward to. Ginger had to think fast to come up with something for lunch.

When the kids came to the cafeteria at lunch, they were delighted with what they found on their trays. Ginger used a triangle sandwich half to make a turkey body and carrot sticks for turkey feathers. She used a small cheese triangle for a beak and an olive slice for the eye. The kids gobbled down Ginger's creative lunch!

Ginger faced a challenge. The food she was going to serve didn't get delivered. Draw a picture below to show what she served the kids instead.

SKILL: Describe how characters respond to major events

THE MAGIC HAT

It was Malik's birthday. His Uncle Ray gave him a hat.

Ray whispered to him, "This is a magic hat. It lets you hear what other people are thinking."

Malik put on the hat and looked at his brother.

His brother thought, "I hope Malik doesn't find out that I took his candy and hid it in my dresser." *Busted!* thought Malik.

Then he looked at his mom.

She was thinking, *I hope Malik will like the bike we have hiding in the garage for him.*

A bike?! thought Malik. He was disappointed that the magic hat had ruined the surprise. Now he'd have to pretend he didn't know about the bike. Malik decided to take the hat off. Maybe he'd find a better use for it someday.

In the text above, underline the answer to each question below using the colors indicated.

1. What two things did Malik do to try out the hat?

2. What was Malik's response to his brother's thought?

3. How did Malik feel after hearing his mom's thoughts?

4. In the end, what did Malik decide to do with the hat?

SKILL: Describe how characters respond to major events

JILL AND THE SUNFLOWER – PART I

Jill lived on a farm. Her mother sent her to the market to sell a cow. They needed the money. On her way there, Jill met an old man.

"I'll trade you these magic seeds for your cow," he said. Jill thought the magic seeds might bring her family the money they needed, so she traded with the old man.

Jill was excited about the seeds, but her mother was not.

"What good will these seeds do us? We needed money!" said Jill's mom. She took the seeds and threw them out the window. The next day, a sunflower plant had grown outside the window. It was so tall, it went up to the clouds. Jill climbed the plant. At the top, she found a sleeping giant.

Continued in Activity 93 . . .

Sometimes characters react differently to the same event. Compare Jill and her mother's reactions to the magic seeds by drawing their faces.

Jill

Jill's Mom

SKILL: Describe how characters respond to major events

JILL AND THE SUNFLOWER – PART 2

Continued from Activity 92...

Suddenly, Jill sneezed! The sleeping giant lifted one eyelid.

"I eat little girls like you as a snack!" he boomed.

Jill quickly climbed to the ground and chopped down the tall sunflower. It came crashing down just as the giant poked his head through the clouds.

"You're lucky you got away!" he yelled.

Jill sat down to catch her breath. She saw the flower from the chopped-down plant. Jill got an idea. She and her mom roasted the seeds from the huge sunflower and sold them. They made up the money they would have gotten from the cow and lived happily ever after.

Many stories follow a pattern. In the exposition, the characters and setting are introduced. In the rising action, the character faces a problem. The climax is the most exciting part of the action. The falling action is the events that lead to the end of the story. The resolution shows how the problem is solved or resolved.

Use words or pictures to fill in the blank boxes below. Look back at the story in Activity 92 if you need to.

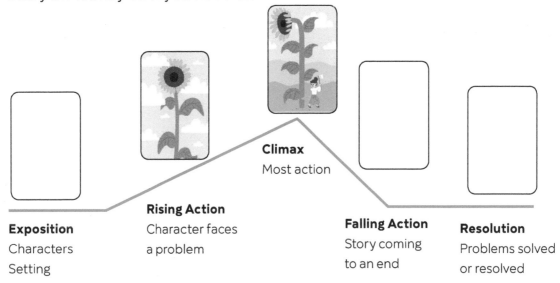

Climax
Most action

Exposition
Characters
Setting

Rising Action
Character faces
a problem

Falling Action
Story coming
to an end

Resolution
Problems solved
or resolved

SKILL: Describe the structure of a story

MRS. PARKER'S PET

Jordan lived in an apartment with his cat, Bruno. One afternoon, Bruno started hissing on the patio. Jordan looked out. There was a lady walking an alligator! She looked up.

"I'm new in the neighborhood. My name is Mrs. Parker and this is Allie," she said. Jordan introduced himself, too.

Every day at four o'clock in the afternoon, Bruno hissed as the alligator walked by. Jordan was tired of the noise. One day, Jordan bought a roasted chicken.

When Mrs. Parker came by with Allie, Jordan said, "I was wondering if Allie would like a snack."

"Sure!" said Mrs. Parker. Bruno watched as Jordan tossed the chicken and Allie chomped it! Bruno ran away and hid. He realized Allie could eat him in one bite. After that, there was no more hissing from Bruno.

Add the following marks to the passage above.

[box]	Draw a box around the exposition (where the main characters and setting are introduced).
____	Underline the rising action (where the character takes on a problem).
☆	Put a star by the climax (the most exciting part of the action).
( )	Put parentheses around the resolution (where the problem is solved).

SKILL: Describe the structure of a story

THE WALK

Below is the same story told by two different characters. Draw a picture of the character that is telling each version.

When Jack sits at my feet, I know he wants to go for a walk. I clip on his leash and he pulls me straight for the door. Jack stops to smell everything in our path. It takes us a long time just to go a couple of blocks with all that sniffing. By then I'm hot and ready to go home.

When I need to stretch my legs, I go sit by Sam. After a while, he gives in and I race him to the door. The best thing about being outside is all the smells! I make sure to stop and sniff the light posts, fire hydrants, and everybody's grass. When Sam gets tired of walking, we head back home.

SKILL: Acknowledge different points of view of characters

RIDING WITH GRANDMA

Draw a line from each statement below to the animal or person who said the words. Parts that are not said by a character are coming from the narrator.

Over summer break, Lucas had to stay with his grandma. He would rather be having fun with his friends.

"Let's go on a bike ride today," said Grandma.

"Where will we go?" asked Lucas.

"I've got a trail in mind," said Grandma.

They rode toward the hills behind her house.

"Wait for me!" said Lucas.

They climbed higher and higher until they made it to the top of the trail.

"This view is incredible!" said Lucas.

"You can see the whole city from up here," said Grandma.

It turned out to be an exciting day after all!

Lucas

Grandma

Narrator

Read the passage again using a different voice for each character.

SKILL: Acknowledge different points of view of characters

ZACK AND JASON

Zack and Jason were twins, but they were very different.

"Come on, Jason! Let's go out. It's a nice day," said Zack.

Jason said, "I'm drawing. The wind will blow away my papers."

"It's more fun to run around outside," said Zack.

"I don't care about running around," said Jason.

"Please? It's no fun to play by myself," said Zack. Then he got an idea. He found some chalk. "You can draw outside with this!" said Zack.

Jason hadn't drawn with chalk in a long time. Outside, Jason quietly worked on drawing a city. He added roads to it. Zack would run in the yard and then stop by and drive his cars on the roads. They each played in their own way, together.

A character's point of view includes what they think or feel about things. Circle the character that matches each thought or feeling below.

1. Quiet activities are the most fun.   Zack   Jason

2. It's better to play outside than inside.   Zack   Jason

3. Running makes me happy.   Zack   Jason

4. It's not fun to play alone.   Zack   Jason

5. I love drawing.   Zack   Jason

SKILL: Acknowledge different points of view of characters

KIARA PRACTICES

Kiara loved playing baseball.

After practice one day, her dad said, "I got a call from your teacher today. She says we need to be working on math facts at home."

"Math facts are so boring!" said Kiara.

"Learning math is important," said her dad. "If you can't find some time to practice math, you'll have to stop playing baseball."

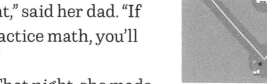

"Not a chance!" said Kiara. That night, she made herself some flash cards and put them in her baseball bag. Before practice and at breaks, she worked on her cards.

A few weeks later her dad said, "Your teacher called again. She said you're really doing well in math!" Kiara gave him a high five, then grabbed her bag for practice.

Each of the sentences below has one incorrect word. Cross out the word that is wrong and write in the correction.

1. Kiara's dad thinks practicing baseball is most important.

2. Kiara thinks math facts are exciting.

3. Kiara's teacher thinks she should spend more time on baseball.

4. Kiara thinks giving up baseball would be fine.

SKILL: Acknowledge different points of view of characters

WHERE CHOCOLATE COMES FROM

Cocoa trees grow in hot and rainy places. These trees grow yellow pods. The pods are the shape of a football. When the pods are ripe, people pick them and slice them open. Inside the pods are cocoa beans. The beans are taken out and baked. Then the beans are ground up, heated, cooled, and made into cocoa powder. You may have seen cocoa powder used in baking. Cocoa powder isn't sweet on its own. Sugar is added to it. The chocolate candy you buy in the store is made from cocoa powder, sugar, and other ingredients. Cocoa beans go through many steps to become a sweet treat.

Read the passage to someone. Then think of questions about the text that start with the words below. Color in a star for each kind of question the other person can answer. See how many stars the other person can get!

| **What** | **Where** | **How** |

SKILL: Ask and answer questions about key details

MAKING SOUND WITH STRINGS

There are many instruments that make sound using strings. All the string instruments shown here can be plucked. This means that a pick or a finger is used to pull the string and then let it go. Plucking the string makes it vibrate, or move back and forth very quickly. This vibration makes sound. Some string instruments, like the violin and double bass, can also be played with a bow. A bow is pulled across the strings, making them vibrate. Long strings, like those on the double bass, play the lowest notes. The violin has short strings, so it plays high notes. A harp can play low and high notes because it has both long and short strings. String instruments can make many different kinds of sounds.

Mark the picture as suggested below.

1. Put a check by the instruments that can be plucked.

2. Circle the instrument that plays the lowest notes.

3. Draw an arrow to the instruments that are played with a bow.

4. Draw a box around the instrument that can play both low and high notes.

SKILL: Ask and answer questions about key details

PLANTING A FAIRY GARDEN

A fairy garden is a miniature garden that looks like it could be home to a fairy. They are perfect if you have only a small space for plants. Fairy gardens can be set up in a corner of a flower bed, under a tree, or in a pot on a patio. It's best to use plants that stay small, like herbs. They will look like miniature trees and bushes in a fairy world. Put moss in a fairy garden to look like grass. Rocks or gravel can be added to create small paths. Some people like to add little benches and houses. Will a fairy garden attract a real fairy? Plant one and find out!

Complete the crossword puzzle using words from the text above.

1. Plants that stay small look like _____ trees.

2. You can plant a fairy garden in a pot on a _____.

3. Moss in a fairy garden looks like _____.

4. Fairy gardens work well in _____ spaces.

5. Make a path out of rocks or _____.

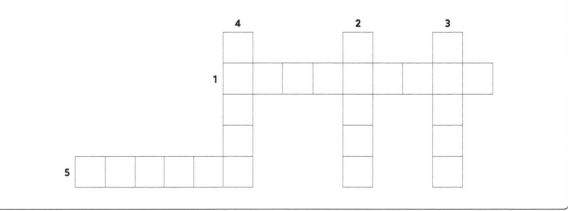

CIRCUS SCHOOL

Many kids take lessons after school to learn things like playing the piano or swimming. Some kids do something a little more unusual. They go to circus school! At circus school, kids can learn how to perform tricks on trampolines and trapezes. They can practice walking on a tightrope and learn to juggle. Some students learn to ride a one-wheeled bicycle called a unicycle. Circus activities help kids improve their strength and balance. Young adults can continue perfecting their skills at professional circus schools. Students study at these schools for about three years. The best performers can get jobs entertaining crowds in shows around the world.

What do you think it would look like inside a circus school? Use details from the passage to draw your answer.

SKILL: Ask and answer questions about key details

MOTORCYCLES AND DIRT BIKES

Motorcycles and dirt bikes are both two-wheeled vehicles, but they have some important differences. Dirt bikes are smaller and lighter. They are made for use on rough roads and tracks. Motorcycles are heavy and made for riding on smooth, flat surfaces. Dirt bike tires are narrow with bumpy treads to grip in the dirt. Motorcycles have tires that are wide and smooth. Dirt bikes have narrow seats and low handlebars. Motorcycles have wider seats for comfort on long rides. Riders must choose the best kind of vehicle for the type of roads or trails they plan to ride on.

Write something that motorcycles and dirt bikes have in common where the ovals overlap. Write something unique about each vehicle in the outer parts of the ovals.

Motorcycles   **Dirt Bikes**

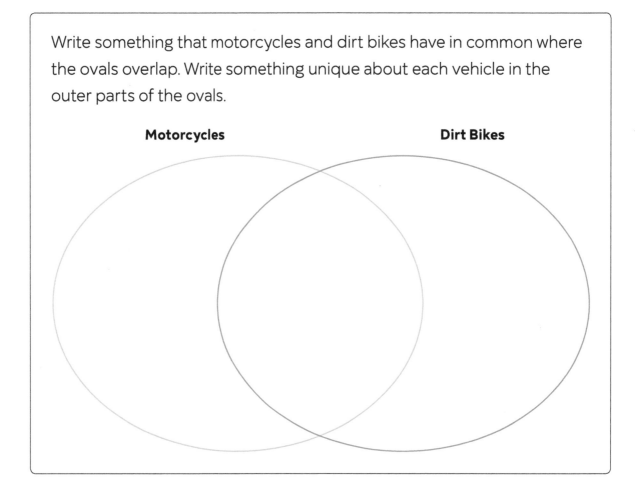

SKILL: Describe connection between two individuals, events, ideas, concepts, or steps

THE RETURN OF THE BISON

Long ago, there were thousands of bison living in North America. Native Americans hunted only a small number of them, so the herds stayed large. Then, settlers began moving into the Great Plains. They started hunting very large numbers of bison. This caused the bison to almost be killed off completely. After a while, people set aside places where bison could be safe. Yellowstone National Park is one of those places. No one can hunt the bison that live there. Yellowstone started with about 20 bison. Over the years, the number of bison in protected places has increased. Today, there are several thousand bison living in Yellowstone.

Use words or pictures to complete each cause and effect relationship in the diagram below.

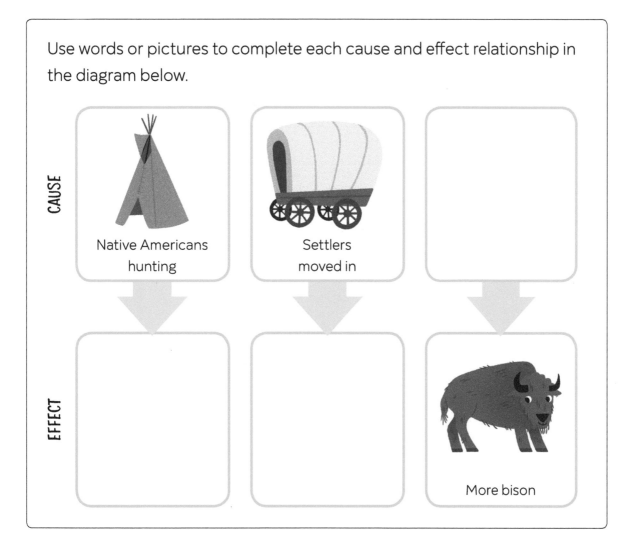

CAUSE

Native Americans hunting

Settlers moved in

EFFECT

More bison

SKILL: Describe connection between two individuals, events, ideas, concepts, or steps

FROM CARRIAGES TO CARS

Long ago, people got around by foot or in horse-drawn carriages. When cars were invented, the roads became more dangerous. Cars were big and fast, and could easily hurt someone. It was clear that we needed ways to control traffic in order to keep the roads safe. One solution was to paint a dividing line down the center of the busiest streets. The line kept cars going in opposite directions from running into each other. The traffic signal was invented to keep cars from crashing in the places where roads came together. Roads have changed to keep up with the invention of cars.

The text describes a problem, and two ways the problem was solved. Use words or pictures to complete the diagram with the problem and the solutions.

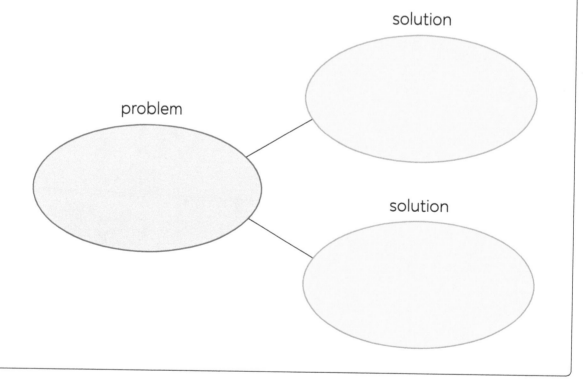

solution

problem

solution

SKILL: Describe connection between two individuals, events, ideas, concepts, or steps

BIRTHDAY CAKE POPCORN

Ingredients

1 bag microwave popcorn

1 cup white chocolate chips

2 tablespoons vegetable oil

3 tablespoons vanilla cake mix

¼ cup sprinkles

Directions

1. Pop the popcorn in the microwave.

2. Mix the white chocolate chips and vegetable oil in a bowl. Heat the mixture in the microwave for 20 seconds and then stir. Repeat until the chocolate is melted. Be careful! It's hot!

3. Stir the cake mix into the melted chocolate.

4. Put the popcorn, chocolate mixture, and sprinkles in a gallon-size bag. Seal and shake the bag until the popcorn is coated.

Recipes like this are a sequence of written steps. In each pair of steps below, circle the one that happens first.

1.
| Melt the chocolate | Pop the popcorn |

2.
| Put the popcorn in a bag | Coat the popcorn |

3.
| Mix the chocolate and oil | Add cake mix |

4.
| Put sprinkles in the bag | Add oil to the chocolate |

SKILL: Describe connection between two individuals, events, ideas, concepts, or steps

MATCH THE STRUCTURE

Each passage below uses a different structure. Read the text and draw a line to match the passage with its structure.

Hopscotch is a fun outdoor game. To play, first you need to draw a line of squares on the ground using chalk. Next, stand on one foot. Finally, try to hop on each square without putting your other foot down.

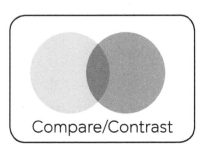

Compare/Contrast

When Earle Dickson's wife got cut, she had to cover the cuts with pieces of cotton held on by tape. Earle invented sticky bandages to make covering cuts easier.

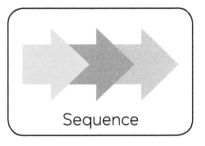

Sequence

Miniature golf and regular golf are both played using a golf ball and clubs. However, mini golf is played on a much smaller course.

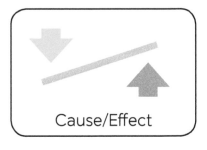

Cause/Effect

Sometimes your location on the Earth is facing the sun, and other times it's turned away from the sun. The rotation of the Earth gives us day and night.

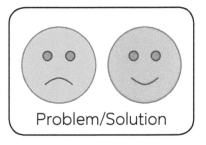

Problem/Solution

SKILL: Describe connection between two individuals, events, ideas, concepts, or steps

PROTECTIVE PATTERNS

Read each focus word below and fill in the stars to show your level of familiarity. Look for clues in the passage about their meaning or ask an adult for help, if needed.

	NEVER HEARD THIS WORD	HAVE HEARD THIS WORD	KNOW A LITTLE ABOUT IT	CAN EXPLAIN IT TO OTHERS
Predator	☆	☆	☆	☆
Conceal	☆	☆	☆	☆
Misidentify	☆	☆	☆	☆

Some animals have special coloring to help them stay safe from predators, or animals that try to eat them. When zebras stand together, their stripes are confusing to predators. It's hard to see where one zebra ends and the other begins. Arctic foxes hide by changing color. In the winter, their fur turns white so they can conceal themselves in the snow. Some butterflies have large spots on their wings that look like big eyes. This causes predators to misidentify the butterflies, thinking they are a much larger animal.

After reading the passage, can you explain the meaning of each focus word to someone else?

SKILL: Determine the meaning of words and phrases

CHINESE NEW YEAR

Chinese New Year is an important holiday in China. The celebrations start at the beginning of the new lunar cycle because the traditional Chinese calendar is based around changes in the moon. Before the holiday, people clean their houses. Once the celebration starts, it is taboo to sweep because it might sweep good luck away. People light fireworks and do dragon dances because it is thought that the loud noise will fend off evil spirits. The Chinese also wear red, give gifts of money to children, and spend time with family. The holiday is celebrated for 15 days and ends with a lantern festival. Chinese New Year is all about starting off the year with good luck.

Draw a line to match each word to its meaning. Use clues in the text to help you.

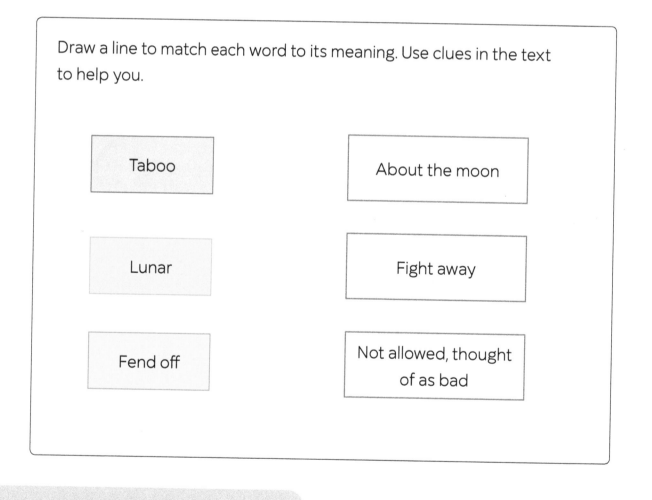

Taboo	About the moon
Lunar	Fight away
Fend off	Not allowed, thought of as bad

SKILL: Determine the meaning of words and phrases

RAINBOWS

To understand how rainbows happen, you need to know a few things about light. The white light from the sun is actually made of many colors of light, called a spectrum. We can't see all the colors when they are together. Light moves from its source to our eyes in waves. Light waves change speed and bend when they move from air to glass or from air to water. This is called refraction. When the path of light bends, the white light breaks apart into different colors. The thick glass of a prism bends light so we can see all of its colors. When we see a rainbow outside, light is passing through raindrops and bending so we can see the full spectrum of colors.

Use the text and the diagram to solve the crossword puzzle.

1. All the colors that are in white light make up a _____.

2. A thick piece of glass that bends light.

3. Another word for light bending.

4. Light moves to our eyes in _____.

SKILL: Determine the meaning of words and phrases

BIRDS OF PREY

Some birds eat small animals. These are called birds of prey. Birds of prey usually hunt for mice, other **rodents**, and insects. They have excellent eyesight and sharp **talons** to catch their **prey**. Hawks, eagles, and falcons are birds of prey that are active during the day. Owls are birds of prey that are **nocturnal**. Birds of prey are fierce animals.

Glossary

nocturnal – active at night

prey – an animal that is hunted by another animal

rodents – a group of animals that includes mice, rabbits, squirrels, rats, and their relatives

talons – the claws of a bird of prey

Use the text and the glossary to determine the meaning of the bold words. Then color the check if the statement is true or the X if the statement is false.

1. Talons are a kind of feather.

2. Hawks and eagles are rodents.

3. Mice and insects are prey for some birds.

4. Owls hunt at night because they're nocturnal.

SKILL: Determine the meaning of words and phrases

TORNADOES

Some words have more than one meaning. Good readers think about which meaning makes the most sense with the text. For each bold word below, color the check by the meaning that makes the most sense.

A tornado is a dangerous weather event. It is a funnel-shaped cloud of spinning winds that stretches from storm clouds down toward the **ground**.	✓ ✓	**Ground** – The land **Ground** – Smashed into small pieces
Tornadoes come from huge thunderstorms called supercells. The most powerful tornadoes have winds up to 200 miles per hour. Tornadoes are frequently **spotted** in the central part of the United States.	✓ ✓	**Spotted** – Having small dots **Spotted** – Seen
This area is nicknamed Tornado Alley because it gets more than 1,000 tornadoes each year. Weather scientists try to predict when a tornado will **strike**. They use sirens and weather alerts to keep people safe.	✓ ✓	**Strike** – Happen **Strike** – When you swing at and miss a ball in baseball

SKILL: Determine the meaning of words and phrases

SNOW ACTIVITIES

Authors write nonfiction to give information, explain steps, or persuade the reader to do or think something. Draw a line from each trophy to the text that deserves it most.

Everyone should try sledding. Sledding is a good way to get some exercise during cold weather because you walk up a hill several times. Sledding is a cheap activity that doesn't require any special skills.

Most Informative
Gives lots of facts

Snowshoeing is an activity you can do in the winter. It involves putting your foot into a wide, flat kind of footwear called a snowshoe. In the past, fur traders and trappers used snowshoes to get through areas of deep snow.

Best Explanation
Tells how to do something

To make a snow angel, first lie on your back in the snow. Then move your arms up and down against the snow. Move your legs apart and back together. Last, stand up and see the angel shape you made in the snow!

Most Persuasive
Gives good reasons for doing something

SKILL: Identify the author's purpose and topic of the text

HERMIT CRABS

Sometimes authors write to answer a question. After each passage, write the question you think the author is answering.

Hermit crabs have five pairs of legs. Some of these legs have claws. The back end of their bodies is covered by a shell. Hermit crabs also have antennae. They can be orange, red, green, or gray.

_____

_____

Part of a hermit crab's body is soft. It could easily be crushed. Hermit crabs find shells to live in to keep themselves safe. When they grow too big for their shell, they find another one to live in.

_____

_____

Hermit crabs are scavengers. This means they do not hunt, but instead eat food that they find. Hermit crabs are known to eat seaweed, dead fish, and rotting wood.

_____

_____

SKILL: Identify the author's purpose and topic of the text

TREES IN THE FALL

During the spring and summer, leaves use sunlight, air, and water to make food for trees. When summer is over, there is less daylight each day. This means leaves are still using up water, but they can't make as much food for the tree. To save water and energy, some trees send a chemical message to each leaf telling them that it is time to fall off. If trees kept their leaves in the winter, the water inside the leaves would freeze and damage them. Then in the summer, the tree would have no working leaves to make more food.

Trees that lose their leaves each year are called deciduous trees. They survive winter by shedding their old leaves and then growing new ones when it is warm again.

Write a word in each blank that explains the author's purpose in writing this passage. Use the shapes to find the letters that complete the last fact.

The author wrote this text to e __ __ __ __ __

why d __ __ __ __ __ __ __ t __ __ __

lose their __ __ __ __ __ __ .

A large oak tree can use __ __ __ h __ __ __ __ __ __

gallons of water a day.

SKILL: Identify the author's purpose and topic of the text

TINY HOUSES

Our communities would be better if everyone lived in their own tiny house. Tiny houses are people-sized but are much smaller than regular houses. Tiny houses have just enough space for people to eat, sleep, and relax. If everyone lived in their own tiny house, there would be more room for outdoor play spaces like parks and trails. People living in tiny houses would have less impact on the environment. Animals and plants would have more space to live. People could grow their own food in gardens with the space that the tiny houses would save. It's time for everyone to downsize to a tiny house.

Draw the kind of community the author is describing in the text. Include details that match the reasons the author gives for living in tiny houses.

SKILL: Describe how reasons support the author's point

THE CASE FOR SUMMER BREAK

Some people think that school should continue during the summer. There are many reasons why it is important for kids to have a summer break from school. Summer break is the best opportunity for kids to explore activities that are not offered at school, such as summer camps. When school is in session, they can spend only a limited amount of time on extra activities. Summer break also gives families a chance to go on trips without kids having to miss school. Finally, kids are ready to work hard and learn after they have had a break. Without a break, both kids and teachers will get burned out. School schedules need to continue to include a summer break.

Answer the questions below by underlining parts of the text in the color indicated.

1. What is the author's opinion about summer break? *Green*

2. What can kids do over summer break that they can't do during school? *Blue*

3. What does the author think would happen if kids went to school all summer? *Yellow*

4. What does the author say some other people think about summer break? *Red*

SKILL: Describe how reasons support the author's point

THE BEST PET

Of all the pets you can choose, fish are the best. Fish don't take up a lot of space. You don't need a yard or a big cage for them. A small aquarium is enough. Fish are relaxing to watch. Some animals have a high level of energy and add chaos to your house. Fish are quiet and calm. If you go on vacation, you can put a fish food block in the tank and the fish will be fine. If you have other pets, you have to find someone to come and take care of them. Cats and dogs can damage furniture and carpets. Fish stay in their tank and don't cause any damage. If you're thinking of getting a new pet, you should get a fish!

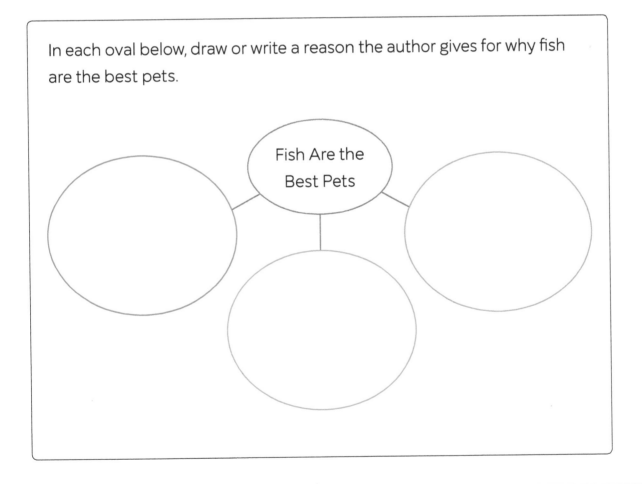

In each oval below, draw or write a reason the author gives for why fish are the best pets.

Fish Are the
Best Pets

SKILL: Describe how reasons support the author's point

SPORTS FOR KIDS

Every kid should spend time playing on a sports team. Playing sports is a good way for kids to get exercise and stay healthy. If kids have sports practices and games to go to, they will spend less time watching TV or playing video games. These things are not active. When kids play on a team, they learn how to work with other people. Teamwork will help kids be successful in their families and jobs when they are adults. Playing sports is a good way to get rid of stress. If kids have had a hard day at school, playing sports is a good way to forget their challenges for a while. If you're not already on a sports team, you should join one.

Fill in the word shapes to explain the author's opinion and supporting reasons.

The author thinks that all kids

should ▢▢▢▢▢ ▢▢▢▢▢▢.

Sports help kids be ▢▢▢▢▢.

Kids learn ▢▢▢▢▢▢▢ when they play sports.

Playing sports helps kids get rid of ▢▢▢▢▢.

ART CLASS FOR ALL

A fact is something that is true and can be proven. For example: Bananas are a fruit. An opinion is how someone feels about something. Other people might feel differently. For example: Bananas are the best fruit. For each statement below, color F if it is a fact or O if it is an opinion.

Schools should offer art class to kids.	F O
When kids are working on art projects, they can improve their fine motor skills. Fine motor skills use the smaller muscles in your hands.	F O
Kids get the chance to express ideas and feelings in art class.	F O
If kids don't get interested in art and choose artistic jobs, our world will look boring.	F O
Art class is a lot of fun.	F O

SKILL: Describe how reasons support the author's point

Answer Key

Activity 1

Underline "Andy" and "bird" in red.

Underline "the grocery store" in blue.

Underline "help to get back outside" in yellow.

Underline "he put small pieces of bread in a line" in green.

Activity 2

Draw the woods in the first frame and a swimming pool behind a house in the second frame.

Activity 3

1. skunk
2. homework
3. downstairs
4. dad

Activity 4

1. false
2. true
3. false
4. true

Activity 5

Possible questions:

Who said the shoes were too expensive?

What did Rico want to buy at the beginning?

When did Rico decide he wanted boots?

Where did Rico see the shoes?

Why did Rico shovel snow?

How did Rico make extra money?

Activity 6

Picture 1 – E

Picture 2 – B

Picture 3 – M

Activity 7

Possible answers:

Picture 1 – painting the box

Picture 2 – adding in the animals

Picture 3 – taking the box to school

Activity 8

Color arrows to the dog with a blanket > the puppy > the dog going out a door > the sleeping puppy > the dog and puppy sleeping

Activity 9

herself, lonely, asked, sharing

Activity 10

Beginning Event – **moves away**

In the beginning, Dustin feels **sad**.

End Event – **joins a club**

In the end, Dustin feels **happy**.

Dustin learns that even though change is hard, it can bring **good things**.

Activity 11

"You'll have to stop playing." (sad face)

They went walking on the tree branches. (nest)

They found a new place to play. (happy face)

Activity 12

Cause 1 – The power goes out.

Effect 2 – Diego feels hot.

Effect 3 – Diego uses the hose to stay busy and cool.

Activity 13

1. Underline "she kicked up some dirt" in red.
2. Underline "The trees are breaking!" in blue.
3. Underline "looked outside" in yellow.
4. Underline "A drop of rain fell on Rick the chick's head" in green.

Activity 14

1. easy
2. faster
3. practice
4. better

Activity 15

wolf

Grandma's

scared

strangers

Activity 16

1. true
2. false
3. true
4. true

Activity 17

Possible answers include: sidewalks, tall buildings, a park, trees, grass, food carts

Activity 18

Include three wheels, an eye on top, a broom arm, and a vacuum slot in the picture.

Activity 19

hot, smoke, buzz, pieces, dirty

Activity 20

1. followed
2. music
3. shed
4. trash

Activity 21

Possible answers include:

Blue whales need . . . water to live in, air to breathe, krill to eat

Blue whales can . . . grow as long as three buses, breathe air, eat krill

Blue whales live . . . in all the oceans, for 80 to 90 years

Activity 22

1. stronger
2. asleep
3. push
4. cells
the heart

Activity 23

1. ~~cooking~~ fires
2. ~~animals~~ tools
3. ~~computers~~ hoses or trucks
4. ~~days~~ months

Activity 24

Write or draw: rabbits, river otters, ants, earthworms, toads

Activity 25

Possible questions:

What –

What makes hot air balloons go up?

What is the fabric part of the balloon called?

How –

How does the air in the balloon get hot?

How does a balloon come back down?

Which –

Which came first, planes or hot air balloons?

Which part of the balloon is at the bottom?

Why –

Why does a balloon need a burner?

Why can't you steer a balloon?

Activity 26

The bars should be labeled from the top down as follows:

cheetah, gazelle, lion, rabbit, human

Activity 27

1. grains
2. 2–3
3. grains
4. no

Activity 28

Circle "Winter Tree Painting" and "Yarn Trees" in yellow.

Circle "Mini Sled" in green.

Circle "Tissue Paper Snow Picture" in blue.

Circle "Ice Pop Stick Snowflakes" in red.

Activity 29

1. false
2. true
3. false
4. true

Activity 30

1. molecule
2. science lab
3. things
4. heat

Activity 31

1. Draw an arrow to the canopy.
2. Circle the forest floor.
3. Draw a star next to the emergent layer.
4. Underline "the understory."

Activity 32

1. seeds
2. green
3. smaller
4. sprout

Activity 33

Reader should draw a cube following the directions provided.

Activity 34

Circle sentences 2, 3, and 5.

Activity 35

1. Draw an arrow to any of the rock surrounding the cave.
2. Circle the pointy rocks (stalactites and stalagmites) shown in the cave.
3. Draw a star on the water.
4. Draw a plant in the ground above the cave.

Activity 36

Possible answers include:
That the dinosaur was a plant eater and that the dinosaur's flat teeth helped grind up leaves and grasses.

Activity 37

Possible answers:

Working dogs have . . . a good sense of smell, the ability to help people

Working dogs can . . . run fast, smell unsafe things, find people, guide people, herd animals

Working dogs need . . . training, love, care

Activity 38

1. false
2. true
3. false
4. true

Activity 39

Answers will vary.

Activity 40

Answers will vary.

Activity 41

Answers will vary.

Activity 42

1. popcorn
2. Florida
3. snow
4. board games
5. ruined

Activity 43

Passage 1 – Wyatt wants to get better at knitting.

Passage 2 – Wyatt doesn't care what Brandon says.

Passage 3 – Brandon realizes knitting is useful.

Activity 44

1. false
2. false
3. true
4. true

Activity 45

1. Underline "Victor" and "mermaid" in red.
2. Underline "by the sea" and "underwater home" in blue.
3. Underline "I miss my family" in green.
4. Underline "I will take you back, but promise to come play by the sea for me" in yellow.

Activity 46

Connect "Somebody" to the picture of Rapunzel in the tower.

Connect "Wanted" to the picture of Rapunzel running free.

Connect "But" to the picture of the witch.

Connect "So" to the picture of Rapunzel and the prince escaping.

Activity 47

Blank 1: Rashad

Blank 2: the same

Blank 3: go to bed

Blank 4: are better for him

Activity 48

cow, animals, paper, disaster, own idea

Activity 49

The first picture should show Lauren feeling scared and the second picture should show her being calm.

Activity 50

Beginning – New neighbors move in.

Middle – Javier waves but the woman doesn't wave back.

End – Javier learns the woman is blind.

Character Change – Javier thought the woman was mean, but learned that she just can't see.

Lesson – Things are not always how they first appear.

Activity 51

Passage 1 – The character feels distracted because of hunger.

Passage 2 – The character is worried about losing something.

Passage 3 – The character is alone and feels sad.

Passage 4 – The character is scared because of a strange sound.

Activity 52

1. basketball
2. clean, room
3. contest
4. fast

Activity 53

Answers will vary.

Activity 54

1. ~~small~~ heavy
2. ~~friend~~ wagon
3. ~~broken~~ being used
4. ~~bounce~~ roll

Activity 55

Include rain, bugs, and a snake in the picture.

Activity 56

Circle "ground/around," "pile/while," "away/stay," "warm/storm," "sky/fly," "deep/sleep."

A gentle rhythm matches this poem because it is about chipmunks getting ready to sleep.

Activity 57

P: Pedro, plops, pot, pitter, pattering, palms (color six squares)

S: splashes, sound, Sal, slides, spoons, slip, slap (color seven squares)

F: fork, flips, flashes (color three squares)

M: My, making, metallic, music (color four squares)

Activity 58

1. false
2. true
3. true
4. true

Activity 59

Circle rhyming words (some are a close rhyme, if not exact) in green: "shuttle/buckle," "tightly/brightly," "eager/speaker," "together/weather," "steady/ready," "gear/atmosphere."

Underline alliteration in blue: "strapped/snugly," "call/count-down," "five/fingers," "hands/hold," "big/breath."

Repeated use of number words simulates the countdown before launch.

The poem has an energetic rhythm that communicates the excitement and nervousness that the astronaut feels.

Activity 60

The feeling checkboxes depend on the opinion of the reader. Likely choices are given here.

Chipmunks Lullaby – Regular Rhythm, Feels Gentle

Cool Clanging in the Kitchen – Irregular Rhythm, Feels Playful, Surprising

Astronaut Blasts Off – Regular Rhythm, Feels Nervous, Energetic

Activity 61

Possible questions:

Who finds Goldilocks?

What gets broken?

When did Goldilocks run away?

Where were the bears?

Why were the bears mad?

How did Goldilocks decide where to lie down?

Activity 62

The reader can just list a few of these:

Bears – bear characters, in the woods, beds

Both – Goldilocks, broken chair, eats food, falls asleep

Sloths – sloth characters, mango, hammocks, Goldilocks never caught

Activity 63

Characters – Partly the same (draw arrow in the middle)

Setting – Different

Problem – Partly the same

Ending – Same

Activity 64

Anansi, food, helping, stir, stretched, Africa

Activity 65

Possible answers:

Venus flytraps need . . . sunlight, soil, water, insects, nitrogen

Venus flytraps can . . . catch insects, close their "jaws," break down insects, get nitrogen from insects

Venus flytraps have . . . leaves that look like jaws, liquid that breaks down insects

Activity 66

Include paintings on the walls, food, clothing, jewels, and weapons.

Activity 67

1. ~~All~~ Some
2. ~~metal~~ wooden
3. ~~birds~~ smoke
4. ~~permanent~~ movable or portable

Activity 68

Possible questions:

Who cleans the dental tools?

What does the dentist do?

Which person would you make an appointment with?

Activity 69

1. seals
2. coldest
3. warmer
4. earlier
5. hunting

Activity 70

Paragraph 1 – Size Records

Paragraph 2 – Speed Records

Paragraph 3 – Life-span Records

Best Title – Animal Record Setters

Activity 71

Big rectangle – Where Energy Comes From

Paragraph 1 – Energy from Oil

Paragraph 2 – Energy from the Sun

Paragraph 3 – Wind Energy

Activity 72

How gorillas look – 3

Facts about gorillas – 1, 2, 3

Gorillas' social lives – 2

What gorillas eat – 1

Activity 73

1. false
2. true
3. false
4. true

Activity 74

dark, prey, electricity, contracts, sandpaper

Activity 75

5 + 7 = 12

17 – 11 = 6

Activity 76

Circle the magnifying glass icon in yellow.

Circle "Flag Football" from the drop-down menu in blue.

Circle "Swimming Pool" on the menu in red.

Circle "HERE" from the main text of the website in green.

Activity 77

1. Add a dot with the current year on the right side.
2. Circle the running machine.
3. Draw a box around the safety bike.
4. Between today's date and 1970, add a dot that says "MB" for mountain bike.

Activity 78

Construction of the Great Wall

Main Topic: The Great Wall of China

Facts: What the wall is made of, What the wall was like long ago, The rebuilding of the wall

A Must-See in China

Main Topic: The Great Wall of China

Facts: What the wall is like today, When to visit the Great Wall, What you can do at the Great Wall, The rebuilding of the wall

Activity 79

Circle the word "bee" or "bees" in each passage in red.

Underline information about bees collecting nectar or about beehives from both passages in green.

Underline any other unique facts from each passage in blue.

Activity 80

Same: topic – pigs

Different: one is about pet pigs, the other is about pigs on a farm (other facts that are unique to each passage would be appropriate here)

Activity 81

1. ~~always~~ never
2. ~~nuts~~ strawberries
3. ~~disgusting~~ delicious
4. ~~hated~~ enjoyed

Activity 82

Jaylene, bus, late, nobody, Saturday

Activity 83

1. animal shelter
2. mess
3. water
4. soft
5. adopted

Activity 84

Example questions:

What did Dax use to help him swim?

Who told Dax that camels don't swim?

Activity 85

Somebody – Underline "Nate" in red.

Wanted – Underline "He hoped his writing would be interesting" in yellow.

But – Underline "Nate had just stayed home" or "he hadn't gone anywhere" in blue.

So – Underline "he built a blanket fort and wrote about all of his imaginary adventures" in green.

Activity 86

trains, loud, study, silent, lot of exercise

Activity 87

Somebody – Tyler

Wanted – to play basketball

But – he broke his leg

So – he came up with plays to help his team instead

Activity 88

1. true
2. false
3. false
4. true

Activity 89

Megan has to give a presentation – External Problem

Megan dresses up – Solution

Megan is embarrassed – Internal Problem

Activity 90

Draw a turkey made from a sandwich triangle body, carrot feathers, cheese triangle beak, and an olive eye.

Activity 91

1. Underline "looked at his brother" and "looked at his mom" in yellow.
2. Underline "Busted!" in green.
3. Underline "He was disappointed" in blue.
4. Underline "take the hat off" in red.

Activity 92

Jill's face should be excited and her mom's face should be angry.

Activity 93

Exposition – The main characters are Jill and her mom. The setting is a farm.

Falling Action – Jill sits down and sees the giant sunflower.

Resolution – Jill and her mom sell sunflower seeds to make money.

Activity 94

Put a box around the first sentence.

Underline where the cat hisses and Jordan buys a chicken.

Put a star by where the alligator eats the chicken.

Put parentheses around the last sentence.

Activity 95

The first picture frame should show a kid and the second picture frame should show a dog.

Activity 96

Over summer … Narrator

"Let's go …" Grandma

"Where …" Lucas

"I've got …" Grandma

They rode … Narrator

"Wait …" Lucas

They climbed … Narrator

"This view …" Lucas

"You can see …" Grandma

It turned out … Narrator

Activity 97

1. Jason
2. Zack
3. Zack
4. Zack
5. Jason

Activity 98

1. ~~baseball~~ math
2. ~~exciting~~ boring
3. ~~baseball~~ math
4. ~~fine~~ bad

Activity 99

Possible questions:

What happens to the cocoa beans?

Where do cocoa trees grow?

How does chocolate get sweet?

Activity 100

1. Put a check by all the instruments shown.
2. Circle the double bass.
3. Draw an arrow to the violin and double bass.
4. Draw a box around the harp.

Activity 101

1. miniature
2. patio
3. grass
4. small
5. gravel

Activity 102

The picture might include a unicycle, tightrope, trapeze, and trampoline.

Activity 103

Possible facts:

Motorcycle: wide seat, heavy

Dirt Bike: narrow seat, light

Both: two wheels

Activity 104

Cause – Native American hunting; Effect – Bison herds stayed large

Cause – Settlers moved in; Effect – Bison were almost killed off

Cause – Places were created to protect bison; Effect – More bison

Activity 105

Problem – Roads becoming dangerous

Solutions – Center dividing line and traffic signals

Activity 106

1. Pop the popcorn
2. Put the popcorn in a bag
3. Mix the chocolate and oil
4. Add oil to the chocolate

Activity 107

"Hopscotch …" – Sequence

"When Earle …" – Problem/ Solution

"Miniature golf …" – Compare/ Contrast

"Sometimes your …" – Cause/ Effect

Activity 108

Predator – an animal that hunts another animal

Conceal – to hide

Misidentify – to get confused about what something is

Activity 109

Taboo – not allowed, thought of as bad

Lunar – about the moon

Fend off – fight away

Activity 110

1. spectrum
2. prism
3. refraction
4. waves

Activity 111

1. false
2. false
3. true
4. true

Activity 112

Ground – the land

Spotted – seen

Strike – happen

Activity 113

Sledding – Most Persuasive

Snowshoeing – Most Informative

Snow Angels – Best Explanation

Activity 114

Possible questions:

What do hermit crabs look like?

Why do hermit crabs have shells?

What do hermit crabs eat?

Activity 115

explain, deciduous trees, leaves, one hundred

Activity 116

The picture should include one or more tiny houses, gardens, parks, trails, and animals.

Activity 117

1. Underline "it is important for kids to have a summer break" in green.
2. Underline "explore activities that are not offered at school" or "go on trips" in blue.
3. Underline "kids and teachers will get burned out" in yellow.
4. Underline "some people think that school should continue during the summer" in red.

Activity 118

Possible answers:

Fish don't take up much space, they are relaxing, you don't have to get someone to take care of them while you're on vacation, and they don't damage things.

Activity 119

play sports, active, teamwork, stress

Activity 120

opinion, fact, fact, opinion, opinion

Skills Index and Common Core Correlations

RL 2.5: Describe the overall structure of a story, including how the beginning introduces the story and the ending concludes the action.

Activity 93: Jill and the Sunflower – Part 2

Activity 94: Mrs. Parker's Pet

RL 2.6: Acknowledge differences in the points of view of characters, including by speaking in a different voice for each character when reading dialogue aloud.

Activity 95: The Walk

Activity 96: Riding with Grandma

Activity 97: Zack and Jason

Activity 98: Kiara Practices

RL 2.7: Use information gained from the illustrations and words in a print or digital text to demonstrate understanding of its characters, setting, or plot.

Activity 16: Keith's Kite

Activity 17: Bots Gone Bad – Part 1

Activity 18: Bots Gone Bad – Part 2

Activity 19: Bots Gone Bad – Part 3

Activity 20: Bots Gone Bad – Part 4

RL 2.9: Compare and contrast two or more versions of the same story (e.g., Cinderella stories) by different authors or from different cultures.

Activity 62: Goldilocks and the Three Sloths

Activity 63: The Gingerbread Man

Activity 64: How the Spider Got Thin Legs

RI 2.1: Ask and answer such questions as *who, what, where, when, why,* and *how* to demonstrate understanding of key details in a text.

Activity 21: Earth's Biggest Animal

Activity 22: Muscles Keep Us Moving

Activity 23: Learning to Fight Fires

Activity 24: What Lives in a Burrow?

Activity 25: All About Hot Air Balloons

Activity 41: The Missing Brownies

Activity 65: Bug-Eating Plants

Activity 66: Pyramids in Egypt

Activity 67: Shelter on the Great Plains

Activity 68: Working in a Dental Office

Activity 69: Life on the Ice

Activity 99: Where Chocolate Comes From

Activity 100: Making Sound with Strings

Activity 101: Planting a Fairy Garden

Activity 102: Circus School

RI 2.2: Identify the main topic of a multiparagraph text as well as the focus of specific paragraphs within the text.

Activity 70: Which Title Works?

Activity 71: Topic Mix-Up

Activity 72: World's Biggest Primates

Activity 73: It Takes More than Pilots

RI 2.3: Describe the connection between a series of historical events, scientific ideas or concepts, or steps in technical procedures in a text.

Activity 103: Motorcycles and Dirt Bikes

Activity 104: The Return of the Bison

Activity 105: From Carriages to Cars

Activity 106: Birthday Cake Popcorn

Activity 107: Match the Structure

RI 2.4: Determine the meaning of words and phrases in a text relevant to a *grade 2 topic or subject area*.

Activity 108: Protective Patterns

Activity 109: Chinese New Year

Activity 110: Rainbows

Activity 111: Birds of Prey

Activity 112: Tornadoes

RI 2.5: Know and use various text features (e.g., captions, bold print, subheadings, glossaries, indexes, electronic menus, icons) to locate key facts or information in a text efficiently.

Activity 26: World's Fastest Animals

Activity 27: Choosing Healthy Foods

Activity 28: Winter Crafts

Activity 29: All About Brazil

Activity 30: What Does a Chemist Do?

Activity 74: Shark Senses

Activity 75: Important Inventions

Activity 76: Recreation Website

Activity 77: Bikes Then and Now

RI 2.6: Identify the main purpose of a text, including what the author wants to answer, explain, or describe.

Activity 113: Snow Activities

Activity 114: Hermit Crabs

Activity 115: Trees in the Fall

RI 2.7: Explain how specific images (e.g., a diagram showing how a machine works) contribute to and clarify a text.

Activity 31: Rainforest Layers

Activity 32: The Oak Tree Life Cycle

Activity 33: How to Draw a Cube

Activity 34: How Much Sleep Do You Need?

Activity 35: All About Caves

RI 2.8: Describe how reasons support specific points the author makes in a text.

Activity 116: Tiny Houses

Activity 117: The Case for Summer Break

Activity 118: The Best Pet

Activity 119: Sports for Kids

Activity 120: Art Class for All

RI 2.9: Compare and contrast the most important points presented by two texts on the same topic.

Activity 78: The Great Wall of China

Activity 79: Honeybees

Activity 80: Places for Pigs

The following activities include comprehension practices that precede and support readers toward understanding Common Core standards in the primary grades, but are not named explicitly within the standards.

Activate prior knowledge

Activity 36: What Can Teeth Tell Us?

Activity 37: Working Dogs

Activity 38: How Crayons Are Made

Make connections to self and the world

Activity 39: The Secrets of Sugar

Activity 40: Antarctica

About the Author

Hannah Braun writes curriculum for teachers and parents of elementary-aged children. She spent eight years as a classroom teacher and has two children of her own. Hannah loves to bring about "A-ha!" moments for kids by breaking down tricky concepts into digestible parts. She holds a bachelor's degree in elementary education and a master's degree in early childhood education. Hannah is the author of the blog *The Classroom Key* (TheClassroomKey.com), where she shares ideas and information about best practices in teaching. In her free time, Hannah enjoys playing French horn in community bands, painting, and taking fitness classes. Follow her on Facebook and Instagram, both @TheClassroomKey.

CPSIA information can be obtained
at www.ICGtesting.com
Printed in the USA
LVHW012359310320
651850LV00011B/113